SCIENCE
and the
SUPERNATURAL

Other books by Aaron E. Klein:

THREADS OF LIFE
TEST TUBES AND BEAKERS
(*with E. H. Coulson*)
TRANSISTORS AND CIRCUITS
(*with W. E. Pearce*)
THE HIDDEN CONTRIBUTORS
BEYOND TIME AND MATTER
SEEDLINGS AND SOIL (*with C. T. Prime*)
ELECTRIC CARS (*with E. John DeWaard*)
YOU AND YOUR BODY

SCIENCE and the SUPERNATURAL
A Scientific Overview of the Occult

Aaron E. Klein

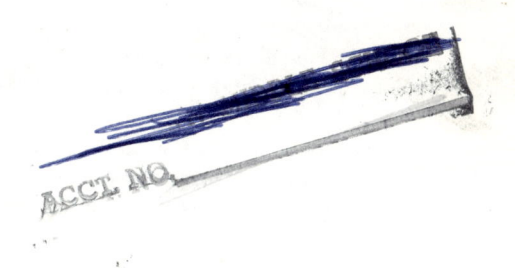

Doubleday & Company, Inc.   Garden City, New York

Library of Congress Cataloging in Publication Data

Klein, Aaron E
Science and the supernatural.

Includes index.
SUMMARY: Discusses psychological, biological, anthropological, and historical reasons for beliefs in supernatural phenomena.
1. Occult sciences—Juvenile literature.
2. Supernatural—Juvenile literature. [1. Occult sciences. 2. Supernatural] I. Title.
BF1411.K575   133
ISBN 0-385-12036-2 Trade
0-385-12037-0 Prebound
Library of Congress Catalog Card Number 76-42339

COPYRIGHT © 1979 BY AARON E. KLEIN
ALL RIGHTS RESERVED
PRINTED IN THE UNITED STATES OF AMERICA
FIRST EDITION

Contents

Stories and Legends — 1

The Possessed and the Obsessed — 12

Vampires, Werewolves, and Such — 54

Witchcraft — 97

Written in the Stars? — 146

Index — 179

SCIENCE
and the
SUPERNATURAL

Stories and Legends

....

ALMOST EVERYBODY IS FASCINATED BY LEGENDS. A legend, after all, is really nothing more than a good story, and everybody likes a good story. Legends are among the best stories, based on things that really happened. Another thing about legends is that the older they are, the better they are likely to be as stories. Time gives the storytellers opportunities to add little details here and there to enhance the dramatic appeal of the tale.

An event was much more likely to be legend material hundreds and thousands of years ago than it is today. Before there were electronic media such as radio and television to send news around the world in seconds, news of events traveled slowly, usually from person to person. As people will do, each teller added his or her own little detail. In time the reality was obscured, although not completely lost, by the wealth of detail and enhancements added by generations of storytellers. Eventually, with the development of writing and printing, legends were written down and printed. So today anyone can go into a library and pick up a book to read legends such as that of Jason and the Golden Fleece, the Norse sagas, and tales of witches, vampires, and werewolves.

Legends have been part of the human scene as long as people have been able to communicate with each other. The earliest men were hunters, and the need for communication, spoken and otherwise, probably grew out of the need to plan and co-ordinate the hunt. Many of the early legends grew out of hunting stories. The same ability to speak that grew out of the need to hunt food successfully also helped to provide the means to relive the excitement of the hunt.

Some twenty thousand years ago, groups of people in Europe went out on well-organized hunts. They pursued animals such as the elephant-like mammoths. Typically, these hunting groups would surround a mammoth and move in on it, carefully, spears at the ready. Suppose that one of the hunters stumbled and fell under the animal. Terrified, the hunter shoved his spear into the hairy elephant's belly. Leaving the spear in the mammoth's belly, the hunter rolled out from under the beast just before it fell to its knees. This development gave the rest of the hunters their chance to move in and finish the elephant off.

That night there was enough meat for a feast. The men, women, and children gathered around an open pit fire, waiting expectantly for the meat to be cooked.

Stories and Legends

After the feast, full stomachs removed the immediate need to get more food, and the people could enjoy a rare period of leisure. Then as now, leisure often meant story time. Today the story often comes out of an electronic box in sound and picture. Back then the story was likely to come from some member of the group who had earned a reputation as a storyteller.

On this night the mainstay was, of course, the hunter who had speared the mighty beast. The storyteller relived the chase for his attentive audience with words and actions, acting out the hunter's fall and thrusting of the spear and imitating the dying elephant with leaps and twists.

Some weeks or months later there was another successful hunt, and again there was a circle of well-fed spectators around the fire. Only, today's hunt had been rather ordinary. Nothing really spectacular had happened. So the storyteller, as he had often done before, drew on a hunt with greater dramatic impact than that day's effort. He retold the story of the hunter who had slipped and fallen under the elephant. This time, however, the storyteller was determined not to lose his audience, so he dressed up his story a little.

The story that was told that evening was not of a clumsy hunter who tripped over his own feet. Now the hunter had become a courageous warrior who bravely, and without regard for his own safety, had charged under the mighty beast and speared it in the underside so that his fellow hunters could easily dispatch it.

Years later, this same storyteller, or perhaps another one in another cave, was again telling of the hunter who speared the elephant's belly. But this time the hunter thrust his spear with such great force that the elephant leaped up into the air and crashed to the ground in a broken heap. And scores or hundreds of years later, cave dwellers might have listened wide-eyed as they were told of a mighty hunter who lifted elephants high into the air on the end of his spear and spun the impaled beasts around as though they were toys. As the years passed, the tales of a mighty hunter who flung elephants high into the air with a flick of a spear captivated listeners. In other versions the great hunter threw elephants across rivers and lakes with his bare hands. And many thousands of years later, in a culture descended from—but much more advanced than—the cave-dwelling hunters, storytellers told of super-strong men with names like Hercules, Prometheus, Samson, and Atlas.

In time, human cultural evolution went beyond hunting into agriculture and the herding of animals. But the end of hunting as the main way of making a living in a culture did not end storytelling. To the contrary—storytelling reached new levels of sophistication. The storyteller gained a new importance in his or her society. Storytelling came to be more than just a source of amusement, a way to pass a few hours. People turned to their storytellers to find out more about the things that were important to them.

There was, indeed, more to man's need to know than just curiosity. His very existence depended on things he did not understand and could not control. A small stream near a settlement, for example, was, most of the time, a giver of water for crops and drinking and a source of fish for food. At times, however, the little stream could become a raging monster sweeping away crops, homes, and people in torrents of water. The sun was a mighty entity that moved in the sky to give light, warmth, and—in some unknown way—life. But the sun could also appear to be a merciless evil that dried up crops and streams to bring starvation and death.

But the storytellers told tales of the sun, water, game animals, and other important things in the environment. These stories were an attempt at understanding. In recounting the mysterious ways of the wind, sun, rain, and other phenomena of nature, the storytellers were doing much more than relating an amusing story. They were exposing and explaining the mysteries. If the storyteller appeared to know so much about these mysterious forces, it followed that he just might have a little more influence with them than the ordinary person. So, in time, the storyteller became an intermediary who could somehow influence the natural forces for the good of the entire society. In some societies, this person might be called a shaman; in others, a medicine man or priest. The shaman (or however he was known) was looked to as someone who could set things right if there was a drought or flood or other misfortune.

As intermediaries who claimed to have the power to intercede with natural forces (or gods), the shamans wielded great power in their societies. They soon developed complicated systems of dealing with natural forces. These varied from simple entreaties to complicated rituals that might involve dancing and the use of paraphernalia in prescribed ways. The intermediaries

Sorcerers would sell anything a gullible buyer might wish for. Here a sorcerer is selling sailors the wind tied up in knots in a rope. (*Woodcut by Olaus Magnus*)

claimed to have the power to intercede with the gods (or whatever else the forces of nature might be called) to prevent catastrophes. These people used many devices, powders, potions, and more in practicing their craft. Of course, the methods of the intermediaries varied from one part of the world to another, but one thing these people all had in common was that they were great storytellers. Like all other storytellers, they did all they could to hold the attention of their audiences. Stories filled with horror, violence, and terror captivated audiences in ancient Mesopotamia as much as similar ones captivate audiences in movie theaters and in front of TV screens today. But any story, as horrible and fantastic as it may be, is based to some extent on something that actually happened. Still, as noted in the saga of the clumsy hunter who became a superman, the events on which the stories are based can be very remote from the story itself.

There soon developed a dualism, or two-sidedness, to the stories told by the priests and the shamans. This dualism was essentially of good and evil. Good things were associated with abundant crops, health, victory over enemies, and general prosperity. Evil was, of course, the opposite. Evil forces brought famine, hunger, disease, defeat, and general lack of prosperity.

Assuming the role of expert in dealing with forces of good and evil, shamans and their counterparts everywhere established favorable positions in their societies. And, as in all societies, as soon as power is established, those who have the power do all they can to hold on to it. As holders of power, the priest class had certain privileges and other advantages. The rest of the people supported them by paying them to do whatever they did to protect them from evil.

The gods and other forces that filled the storytellers' tales were powerful entities that literally held the power of life or death over ordinary people. These strange, mysterious, but powerful forces had to be pleased. They could not be crossed lest the people suffer dire consequences. Through experience and what the shamans told them, the people learned what to do and what not to do. The shamans and priests spelled out the proper behavior for everyone. Straying from the proper behavior could bring disaster to the whole group, particularly the transgressor. The shamans drew on their best storytelling talents to let the people know what would happen if there were violations.

Of course, the telling of stories has never been limited to "official" storytellers. People have always told stories to each other. The swapping of stories by people everywhere speeds up the change in these tales until it is impossible to tell what is the original event on which the story was based.

Frequently the stories that made up the lives of ordinary people were far more interesting than those put out by the "establishment." Often the storytellers-turned-priests-or-shamans forbade the telling of any version but their own. On the other hand, the people's own stories—that is, folklore—was frequently incorporated into the establishment's official line. This was particularly so if one establishment took over from another. For example, as Christianity spread through Europe, the belief and practices of the people eased the way for Christian doctrine. To Christians, whatever was non-Christian was pagan or heathen. Evergreen trees, mistletoe, and holly wreaths were important elements in various pagan European religions. Incorporating these things into the celebration of Christmas helped to convert the pagans to Christianity.

Folk tales all over the world are filled with horrible, terrible, but fascinating creatures, human, half-human, and animal. There are certain similarities between these creatures in different parts of the world. There are demons in the folklore of Europe, Africa, and the Far East. There are tales of witches in Africa that rival the more familiar witch stories of Europe for sheer entertainment value.

This rather unhappy eighteenth-century sorcerer has been condemned to death by the Inquisition. If he were indeed a sorcerer, it seems that he would have conjured up a way out of his predicament.

The vampires, werewolves, witches, demons, and other horrors were very real to many people hundreds of years ago. People lived in paralyzing terror of these horrible creatures. To many, a vampire or witch was not just a device to make a story interesting but a real object that truly existed and could actually harm or kill people.

It is easy for us to dismiss belief in things such as vampires and werewolves as unscientific. To be "scientific," a conclusion must be based on valid evidence. However, before the advent of experimental science, people had ways to explain things that were just as valid to them as scientific methods are to us. To the ancient Greeks, for example, a hailstorm was one of the ways in which the god Zeus showed his anger. To a modern meteorologist, a hailstorm occurs when an upward air current brings droplets of water into high, cold atmospheric layers where the droplets freeze. This can happen again and again, and the more often it happens, the bigger the hailstones are likely to be. Of course, the partisans of Zeus can come right back and say the upward air currents are just one more way Zeus can show that he is angry.

In this age of science, there are still people in the world today who *really* believe in the existence of things such as vampires and witches. There are areas of the world, such as the Mato Grosso rain forest of Brazil, where truly primitive people still live. Although they have had some contact with people from the industrialized, civilized world, they live their daily lives in their own world, one of demons and spirits. But such beliefs are not limited to primitive people. There are still thousands of people in Europe, for example, who smear garlic on their doors and window sills to keep vampires away. This sort of practice, although largely found in relatively isolated areas such as mountain villages, is by no means restricted to such places.

Even those of us who do not openly confess to such

beliefs are influenced by them. People will often say, "What possessed him to do a thing like that?"—implying that something such as a demon possessed the body and mind of whoever did "something like that."

As was implied in the story of the clumsy hunter who became a hero, there are few stories in the human repertoire that are not based, however remotely, on some actual person or event. In this book we will take a look at some natural, explainable phenomena that could well have been the basis of many of the popular tales about vampires, werewolves, witches, and other so-called supernatural beings and events that have horrified and entertained us for thousands of years.

Almost all of the legends we will consider here came out of Europe and the Middle East. There are, of course, many fascinating legends and myths from all parts of the world. But the witch and vampire lore we are likely to read about and the tale of demonic possession we might pay to see dramatized at the movie theater are all most likely to be based on legends that came out of Europe. And strangely or sadly enough, there are many people in the civilized world today who see these stories not as entertainment, which is all they are intended to be, but as real events.

The first supernatural phenomenon we will consider is possession, the subject of current top money-making films that far too many people took so seriously that they refused to be entertained.

The Possessed and the Obsessed

Master, my son is possessed by a mute spirit. Whenever this spirit attacks him, he throws him to the ground and torments him with convulsions. Then the boy grinds his teeth, foams at the mouth, and becomes quite parched.

Mark, 9:17

The patient has tonic (without relaxation) seizures. Seizures may be accompanied by clenching of the teeth and excessive salivation. The tongue may be bitten during the seizure and the patient is usually incontinent during the seizure. Unconsciousness, cyanosis, falls, and injuries from the falls may occur. The patient has amnesia during the attack and may be confused and disoriented afterward.

Description of a grand mal seizure

THE SECOND STATEMENT IS A DESCRIPTION of a grand mal epileptic seizure. The first quotation may also be a description, from the New Testament, of a grand mal epileptic seizure. To many people, the biblical account is far more interesting reading than the second, which is written in the style of a twentieth-century medical textbook. Despite the difference in language, a similarity between the two passages is obvious.

There have been epileptics (people with epilepsy) for many thousands of years. There are different types of epilepsy, characterized by seizures of one kind or another. Some seizures are so mild that they are nothing more than a brief loss of awareness, unnoticed by people around the victim. Others, such as grand mal, involve violent "fits" in which the victim loses consciousness, thrashes about wildly, foams at the mouth, and so on. The exact cause of epilepsy is not known. It is not thought to be directly inherited, although there is some evidence that a *tendency* to have epilepsy may be inherited in some way that is not yet known. There is also some evidence that epilepsy may be caused by a bad head injury or diseases such as spinal meningitis. The brains of epileptics produce certain types of electrical activity that can be detected with an electroencephalography machine. In the use of an electroencephalography machine, tiny wires are attached to the scalp. These wires pick up tiny electrical currents from the brain. The machine converts the currents into wavy-line patterns on a recording instrument. Doctors can read these lines and get information on a number of brain conditions, including epilepsy. Epilepsy cannot usually be cured, although it can be controlled through various drugs. Thousands of epileptics are now able to lead normal lives and go for many years without having a seizure.

Of course, there were no encephalography machines, or any way of treating epilepsy, such as with drugs, when the biblical passage that begins this chapter was written. As suggested by the medical-book-style paragraph, seeing a grand mal seizure can be a pretty upsetting experience for someone who doesn't know what it's all about. Fifteen hundred years ago, you can be sure no one knew what epilepsy was all about. People in different parts of the world had a variety of explanations for epileptic seizures. Descriptions of the behavior of certain Egyptian pharaohs indicate that they might have had epilepsy. These accounts, written thousands of years before the New Testament, also suggest that the epileptic seizure was believed to be some kind of religious experience—a communication with spirits or gods. Mohammed, the founder of the Moslem religion, probably had epilepsy, which no doubt contributed to the awe with which his followers regarded him.

The father of the afflicted boy in the biblical passage complained that his son was *possessed* by something. Possession by spirits, demons, of one type or another was, of course, an eminently logical, sensible way to explain such things as epileptic seizures. The word *epilepsy* comes from a Greek word that means "to seize or possess," and attacks are still called seizures. But before we can smugly dismiss our ancestors as superstitious fools, we have to look at the way epileptics were treated in the recent past in our culture and still are treated in many parts of the world, including the United States. As late as the present century, epileptics were considered to be insane and were often put in insane asylums or worse. They were also regarded as retarded, and many were placed in institutions for the mentally retarded.

As a group, epileptics are no more likely to be mentally retarded or mentally ill than anyone else. Many famous, accomplished people were epileptics. Feodor Dostoyevsky, the great Russian novelist, was epileptic. In his novel *The Idiot* he vividly described what it felt like to go through an epileptic seizure. Julius Caesar was an epileptic, and he did not let the disorder keep him from going out into the field with his troops or from being ruler of the Roman world.

Despite ample proof that epileptics can live normal lives, there are still laws in some states that restrict the rights of epileptics to drive an automobile and hold certain types of jobs. And even where there are no discriminatory laws, lives of epileptics and their families are often made miserable by the fear and lack of understanding of other people.

In the Western world, the idea that epileptics were possessed by demons caught hold in the Middle Ages. Historians classify the Middle Ages as roughly the period from the decline of Rome to the fourteenth century. Historians may disagree about the exact dates, and some people refer to this time as the "Dark Ages." The Catholic Church had a great deal of power in those days. The day-to-day lives of most people were controlled by the Church in a much more direct way than is the case today. The threat of eternal punishment after death for those who did not obey the rules was very real to many people. And death was never very far away in the Middle Ages. In the 1300s, bubonic plague—the Black Death—swept through Europe, killing off a fifth of the population.

Although the fear of going to hell and being subjected to the none-too-tender mercies of the Devil and his "assistant demons" was very real, one did not have to wait for death to be tormented by demons and such. It was generally believed that demons or the Devil himself could come up, out of hell, and enter the bodies of people and stay awhile.

The Devil was the very personification of evil, and although the concept of the Devil reached a high level of refinement in the Middle Ages, it was even then very old. The idea of the Devil, or Satan, evolved from the division between good and evil that humans developed to explain phenomena that were beneficial and those that were harmful. The Western or Christian ideas of the Devil were taken from the Hebrew, which in turn borrowed heavily from Persian religions. In the ancient Persian religion, the good god was called Ormazd, and the evil god, Ahriman. Whatever good Ormazd did, Ahriman busily tried to undo. If Ormazd made the newly sown crops good, Ahriman was not far behind doing what he could to make them bad. In one of the Persian stories, Ahriman disguises himself as a snake to carry out some of his most treacherous deeds. The parallel between the Persian story and the role of the snake in the story of the Garden of Eden seems obvious, although in the Hebrew version the snake is a real snake acting as the agent of the evil forces rather than the evil force (the Devil) itself.

The Possessed and the Obsessed

A medieval representation of the Devil as a trumpeter of evil.

The word *Satan* comes from a Hebrew word that means "adversary" or "accuser." It seems that the original concept of Satan was quite different from the one that developed in the Middle Ages. In the Hebrew tradition, Satan was an angel with a special duty. His mission was to accuse earthly men of misdeeds of one kind or another. He could be regarded as a symbolic guilty conscience. It was Satan's further duty to prosecute the accused at a sort of heavenly tribunal. In this role, he could be thought of as the prosecuting attorney. Note that this concept of Satan does not have Satan leading people into evil ways. He merely sees to it that those who do transgress get what's coming to them.

But gradually the concept of Satan began to change. He was, for a time, represented as a very suspicious character who trusted no one and expected the worst of everybody. Satan was seen as a particularly bothersome nuisance. Eventually he came to be regarded as the most dangerous enemy of humankind.

Later religious thought has Satan and a group of colleague angels banished entirely from heaven, from whence he went down to hell to carry out his dirty work. By the time the Christian Church had become established in Europe, a clear conflict between good and evil, represented by God and the Devil respectively, had emerged. And while God had his angels to help him with his work, Satan had his helpers, too—the demons.

The idea of demons is by no means exclusive to Christian thought; it seems to be fairly widespread over much of the world. When Christian missionaries came to Europe they found that the local pagans had a rich demon supply of their own. Persians and other peoples of the Middle East believed in spirits of darkness, or jinn. These jinn were capable of carrying out all kinds of malicious acts. The jinn idea has come down to us in characters from *Tales of the Arabian Nights* called genies. Under the right circumstances, and with the

A late-fifteenth-century woodcut showing the Devil taking away a child that has been sold to him.

proper magic, genies could be made to do the will of people. In Arabian genie stories, usually only sorcerers with the right powerful magic can control genies. However, the storytellers of that time knew even then that people like to identify with characters in the story, and so we have tales such as "Aladdin and the Enchanted Lamp," in which a common person gets control of a genie through the medium of possessing a lamp, and the sorcerer is beaten at his own game. If one loses control of a genie, it can do all kinds of awful things to its erstwhile master.

The ancient Greeks had demons in their religion and, indeed the word *demon* itself is Greek. But the Greek *daemon* was not evil. Rather, the daemon was more like the Christian guardian angel. At birth, each person was given a daemon by the chief god of the Greeks, Zeus.

The Christian concept of Satan is much more like that of the Persian Ahriman than the Hebrew idea of Satan. Like Ahriman, the Christian Satan is waging active warfare against man. And, like Ahriman, he commands an army of demon helpers.

Many writers of the Middle Ages were very specific in their discussions of demons. There were certain demons with names, and one demon was portrayed as being nastier and meaner than another. There were low-order demons and high-order demons, rich demons and poor demons, weak ones and strong ones.

In the minds of medieval people, demons were very real in their own particular way. Although they were regarded as spirits that could be invisible and pass

This fifteenth-century woodcut shows a group of demons around a sleeping man, urging him to commit all manner of sins. The sins are written in Latin in the bannerlike strips near the demons. The voice banners are similar to the voice balloons of comic strips.

The Possessed and the Obsessed

through walls, keyholes, and so on, they could also assume definite forms. The form most often represented was that of an animal.

Eastern, Western, and "primitive" religions all represent demons in animal forms, of one kind or another. Christian demons were often pictured as having hoofs, tails, and horns. They could have basically human forms with a human face, but might have hoofs or birds' feet or a combination of these. Or they could have the face of an animal such as a lion, the body of a man, and the hoofs of a goat. They could also have wings. Most often, however, they were pictured as having human hands. They needed hands to carry out their evil deeds. These demons were believed to stream forth in great numbers from the depths of hell, especially at night, to wreak all kinds of havoc.

Demons were thought to be strange, fearful things and so, if they looked like anything, they could not look exactly like humans. The picturers of demons drew on what they knew: animals. Animals were (and still are) very important to people. They can provide food, but they can also be dangerous. Sometimes people were attacked by wild animals, although probably not as often as stories of such attacks might make one think. Of course, the most important aspect of animals was the hunt. Drawings of people dressed in animal skins have been found in caves. These pictured people were probably shamans, who dressed in the animal skins and did some kind of dance in order to invoke animal spirits in a favorable way.

A representative group of demons. From left to right: Amduscias, a trumpet player; Lucifer; Ronwe, who provided knowledge of languages; Orobas, the horse-headed prince of hell; Ukobach, who gave the world fried foods; Xaphan, who fanned the fires of hell; and Eurynome, the prince of death. The illustrations appeared in Collin de Plancy's *Dictionnaire Infernal*, a widely read work on demonology.

So animals were, at the same time, objects of fear and of veneration. They were feared as sources of injury and death and venerated as sources of food and other necessities. The animals concept applied to the unknown and fearful went beyond demons into werewolves, and vampires, and similar sinister flying things. But to most common people in the Middle Ages, demons and such were more than just concepts—they were very real, even to those who never claimed to have seen a demon or anything of the kind. And among the terrifying types of havoc they were thought to be capable of was possession.

It was thought that when a demon got tired or thirsty or just felt like being ornery or mischievous, it could enter the body of a person and possess that person, body and mind. It was also thought that you could

The Possessed and the Obsessed

tell if a person was possessed by the peculiar way the possessed acted. Demons could cause their victims to writhe, scream, convulse, soil themselves, and utter strange sounds. If these symptoms sound familiar, it might be because they are the very same as the symptoms of an epileptic seizure.

But if a demon did take possession of someone, all was not lost. There was exorcism. Exorcism is a rite, ritual, or method of some kind designed to get the demon to leave. Some of these methods could be quite drastic. The phrase "beat the devil out of him" alludes to one such.

A French woodcut of the sixteenth century showing a priest exorcising a demon from a woman.

There have actually been epidemics of possession. When there are epidemics of anything—that is, when one particular disease or condition happens again and again to many people in a relatively short period of time—the obvious thing is to look for something that is causing the problem. One of the more celebrated cases of "mass possession" occurred in 1633 among the nuns at a convent in Loudun, France. Although the supposed mass possession took place in 1633, the description of the events was not formally written up until 1839. According to the account of the mass possession, some of the nuns started to babble strange, nonsensical sounds.

Several exorcists were called in. One result of the incident was that a priest was accused of making arrangements with the Devil for the nuns to be possessed by demons. The offending demons were even named. Among the accused demons were Asmodeus, Sabulon, and one called Astaroth, who was reputed to be a particularly powerful and troublesome demon. The priest, Urbain Grandier, vigorously denied any contact with the Devil or demons, but, according to the 1839 account, one of the demons turned "state's evidence." According to the priest's accusers, the demon, Asmodeus, broke into the Devil's cabinet, stole the pact that Urbain Grandier had signed with the Devil, and gave the pact to the prosecution. The prosecution claimed that the pact was notarized by the "chief devil and the lords and princes of hell." Protesting his innocence to the end, Urbain Grandier was burned at the stake, but only after being horribly tortured.

Sister Jeanne des Anges, the mother superior of the Loudun convent, supposedly possessed because of the demonic dealings of Urbain Grandier.

The "contract" between Grandier and various members of the hell "establishment," including Beelzebub, Astaroth, and Elimi. It is written backwards, because it was widely believed that demons read backwards.

The Possessed and the Obsessed

Urbain Grandier's death did not end reports of possession in the convent. One of those said to be possessed, Jeanne des Anges, reported in her autobiography:

> At the outset I was in a disturbed mental state for three whole months. . . . The Devil confused me to such an extent that I could hardly separate his desires from my own. . . . On the way to Communion the Devil seized my hand and made me throw the half-moistened Communion wafer I had received into the priest's face. I am certain I did not do this of my own free will.

If the mass behavior of all the nuns in the convent was similar to that described by Jeanne des Anges, one possible explanation could have been a fungus that infects rye, an important food grain. Two hundred years ago, rye was a much more important grain crop than it is today. Rye, like most other plants, can become diseased. One of the more common diseases of rye is infestation with a fungus called ergot. Any plant disease affecting a food crop is in itself a problem. The disease reduces the crop yield. Money has to be spent on sprays and other treatments and, in the end, everyone pays more for the crop and the food made from it. Ergot, however, can be much more than just a disease of plants. If it is eaten by people, all kinds of unpleasant things can happen. And since rye is a food plant, ergot is quite likely to be eaten and, indeed, has been eaten many times.

A scene showing Urbain Grandier being burned at the stake. This seventeenth-century woodcut shows exorcism scenes at the left, and to the right some of the "possessed" nuns are carrying on.

Eating ergot can result in a disease called ergotism. Depending on the type of ergotism the victim has, the symptoms can range from dizziness to hallucinations to the rotting away of fingers, hands, and even arms and legs. The latter kind of ergotism is called gangrenous ergotism. Epidemics of gangrenous ergotism occurred in Europe around a thousand years ago. Among other things, it was called *ignis sacer*, the holy fire. It was also called St. Anthony's fire; victims prayed to St. Anthony for relief.

The other type of ergotism is convulsive ergotism. The symptoms suggest that this condition may have been the basis for stories of possession and other "distempers" and "afflictions" generally thought to be the work of the Devil, his demons, and witches. The victim experiences dizziness, ringing of the ears, crawling and tingling feelings in the skin, disordered senses, and vomiting. In many cases the victims have violent fits and painful muscle spasms. There are also usually hallucinations. That is, the victim "sees things" that aren't really there or "sees" gross exaggerations of objects, people, colors, and so on. The pain of the muscle spasms and the terror of hallucinations may cause the victim to scream and yell. The victim might flail about, jerking and kicking wildly. People "tripped out" on LSD have reported similar symptoms, a circumstance that is quite understandable. LSD is made from ergot. The substance in ergot that causes the hallucinations and other symptoms of convulsive ergotism is indeed LSD, short for lysergic acid diethylamide.

Biblical and later descriptions of possessed and bewitched people could also have been inspired by epileptic fits. However, it is quite likely that accounts of possession of whole towns, monasteries, or nunneries, such as the one in Loudun, were descriptions of ergotism. Groups of people living together in places like monasteries are likely to buy their bread or flour from the same baker or miller. This was especially the case in a small town of medieval times and even more recently. Ergotism was widespread in France in the 1600s, and since a convent was likely to procure its flour from one source, it is quite conceivable that the nuns at Loudun obtained a large consignment of ergot-infected flour. Since the major account of the events was written over two hundred years after they occurred, details are bound to be hazy and confused. There is, again, the tendency of the storyteller to embellish a little here and there to make a better story. The account of the demon providing the needed evidence is in the best tradition of a good detective story. Similar plots can be seen on TV almost any evening.

Despite the efforts of the exorcists, the nuns continued to act in a way that made them appear to be possessed, long after Grandier's death. Eventually their behavior returned to normal, in all probability because the convent's supply of ergotized flour had run out, and once they had returned to normal, they were declared to be exorcized.

Why didn't the entire population of the town in which the convent was located also exhibit the symptoms of ergotism? One possibility is that the nuns may have bought their flour from a source that was not the same as the one that supplied the village. Some convents depended on charity for all or part of their food. A miller might have been more disposed toward giving away diseased flour than wholesome flour. Of course, in the seventeenth century, the miller would not have known anything about ergot. But he would have noticed that some batches of flour were darker than others. Ergot is black, and flour made from ergot-contaminated grain has a definite grayish appearance. The miller might have had trouble selling such flour, so he would have given it away, quite likely to some religious institution such as a convent, and, in so doing, brought grace to his soul.

Some orders of nuns and priests had rules that forbade them to take from others. The members of such orders might have raised their own food crops, includ-

An incident similar to that of Loudun occurred at Aix-en-Provence in France in 1611. One nun became hysterical and accused a priest, Louis Gaufridi, of bewitching her and causing her to become possessed. This hysterical behavior spread to other nuns in the convent.

ing rye and other grains that could have become infested with ergot.

Whether or not ergot was actually the cause of the strange events in Loudun in 1633 can never be proved or disproved. However, a comparison can be made with a much more recent series of events that were definitely linked to ergotism. These also occurred in France, in 1951 in the town of Pont-St.-Esprit.

In the summer of 1951, the entire town of Pont-St.-Esprit seemed to go mad. It started around the middle of August, and one of the first suggestions of the strange events that were to rip apart this little Rhône Valley town came from a cat that went crazy. The cat belonged to some people who kept a vineyard just outside the village. On August 17, 1951, the cat howled and writhed in agony. It had convulsions, clawed at the air, screamed horribly, and soon fell to the floor, dead. The cat had shortly before eaten a meal composed largely of food left over from the family's dinner table.

On the night of August 17, many people in Pont-St.-Esprit started to feel strange. Many had upset stomachs, and quite a few had chills and nausea. Of course, at the outset, each family thought that it alone was having these problems. It had no way of knowing that families all over the village and the surrounding countryside were having the same problems.

The first person to get an idea that the sickness was town-wide was a doctor who, as soon as he returned from a vacation, started to get an unusually large number of calls about upset stomachs and similar complaints. When the doctor returned from his house calls, he found his office filled with people complaining of the same symptoms. There was nothing the doctor could do other than prescribe the usual remedies for upset stomachs. The next morning many of the patients phoned to report that they felt much better. The doctor thought the epidemic of indigestion was over.

Early that morning, he answered a frantic house call request. A woman in the household was having terrible convulsions. Her mouth foamed, and her face was twisted in such a way that even members of her own family could hardly recognize her. The doctor would make many more house calls that day, and in each home he found another set of horrors.

In one home he found a man who had been running around the yard like a madman. The man ran back into the house, huddled under the blankets, and shrieked alternately that he was burning up or that he was freezing. After several of these calls, the doctor felt he should inform the mayor. But news of the mass sickness had spread through the town and the mayor already knew what was going on. Reports of sickness kept coming in, and the doctor had more than he could handle. Calls for help went out to other towns.

On Sunday night, August 19, the main street of Pont-St.-Esprit was filled with people who had left their homes because they could not sleep. They gathered in knots to talk about their sickness. But their talk of sickness was not somber and serious. It was light and frivolous. The people were laughing, giggling, and acting in a way that could be described as silly. Worse was yet to come.

About one-thirty Monday morning, the doctor went on another house call. The patient was a five-year-old girl. The girl was having severe convulsions and screaming that tigers were in the room, that they were going to bite her. The little girl was not the only victim in the household. The girl's father was moaning that he just had to get curtains with beads on them for the flies.

The doctors in the town continued to be faced with situations they had never before encountered. One woman threw pots at the hapless doctor who came to treat her. She later said she had thought the doctor was a skeleton dressed in a black suit. Another man ran from his house screaming that his enemies were going to kill him. He ran back to his house, piled furniture against the door, and stationed himself at a window armed with a shotgun. An eleven-year-old boy suddenly attacked his mother, beating and scratching her. The boy's father could not help. He was in bed hallucinating, in convulsions. Another man tore his bed to pieces, thinking the whole time he was a circus strong man performing before an applauding audience. The calamity continued to grow. But it was not until the night of August 24, 1951, that the entire town erupted into one of the most unbelievable scenes in modern French history.

A man named Charles Vadadaire, one of the sleepless people who had gathered on the town's main street, screamed and started to run down the street. His friends followed him, trying to calm him, but he yelled at them to stay away, screaming that he had snakes in his stomach and they were burning him. He ran to the edge of a river and would have jumped in had he not been tackled by one of his friends. The man seemed to have superhuman strength, breaking away from his friends several times before they managed to get him to the hospital.

The scene at the hospital was right out of a horror movie. The halls shook with the screams of the afflicted. One Joseph Puche, a retired airline pilot, was brought into the hospital, gasping for breath. He was placed in a room on the second floor. A few minutes later he was seen standing at the window, waving his arms wildly. He called out, "I'm an airplane and I can fly!" He jumped from the second-floor window, his arms outstretched as if they were airplane wings. He landed with a thud, breaking both legs. He got up and ran at a good rate of speed down the street on his shattered legs. He was caught, but it took several men to restrain him and bring him back, still protesting that he was an airplane, to the hospital.

All night long the afflicted were brought screaming into the hospital. There was the man who insisted that bandits with donkey ears were after him. A woman begged the doctors not to come near her or the flames roaring out of her fingers would burn them. Some victims sat quietly in what they believed to be deep religious or spiritual experiences. Oddly enough, almost all the victims, even the ones who screamed the most, had moments of lucidity and calm. But they would soon start again, alternating between periods of convulsions and hallucinations and complete calm.

Although medical teams were sent in from other cities to help, there were not enough people to take care of all the victims. Some escaped, running out into the streets. Some of the victims had physical symptoms. Many had gangrene on the feet and legs, a slow rotting or deterioration of the flesh. In the mass confusion, a pattern began to emerge. Visions of animals, such as lions, tigers, and snakes, were very common. Also quite prevalent was the urge to jump out of windows. And the occurrence of gangrene made many doctors in attendance suspect that ergotism was the cause of the nightmare they were going through.

Months passed before all the victims recovered to any great degree. Some of them died. For many, the recovery did not come quickly. The general pattern was that the periods of lucidity and rational behavior would last longer, alternating with shorter periods of hallucinations. Others recovered rather quickly.

As the victims recovered, the long investigations into the cause of Pont-St.-Esprit's nightmare dragged on. The bakers of Pont-St.-Esprit reported that on the day before the troubles started they had had problems with the batch of flour they had received. The flour was of very poor quality. It was grayish, and the dough made from it was gray, greasy, and difficult to work. But they made the bread from the flour, and the villagers, as usual, bought it and used it for their meals.

At the time, the bakers had little to say about where they bought their flour. Flour was distributed by what was essentially a monopoly, operated with government support. The bakers had to accept whatever flour was shipped to them. The ergot-infected flour had come from one of the warehouses operated by the giant flour distributing company. The bakers could not complain to the miller who had made the flour. Indeed, they had no idea who the miller was. The millers sold their flour to the distributor, not to individual bakers. If the bakers rejected a shipment, they might have to go for days without flour, something they could not do if they hoped to stay in business. As it turned out, the flour that was shipped to most of the bakers in Pont-St.-Esprit in mid-August 1951 had come from one mill. The system of distribution that was in effect determined that the Pont-St.-Esprit bakers would receive the gray flour.

Eventually, after months of legal hearings, filled with contradictory evidence, it was conclusively proved that the flour was infested with ergot and the result had been an epidemic of ergotism, both convulsive and gangrenous. A plague from the Middle Ages had come to modern France. Epidemics of ergotism had swept through Europe many times in medieval times, and there had been a large outbreak of ergotism in Russia in the mid-1700s.

There was plenty of medieval-style hysteria in Pont-St.-Esprit in 1951. Quite a number of people who had not eaten the contaminated bread also went berserk. People were overcome with fear, wondering if they would be next, or if someone they loved—a child, wife, husband, sweetheart—would suddenly turn into some kind of monster. People walked through the streets clutching rosaries and crucifixes. It was indeed as if the Middle Ages had visited the twentieth century. If all this had happened in the same village or elsewhere in Europe in the Middle Ages, the cry of "Possession" and "It's the Devil's work" would certainly have been heard.

As soon as the people of the village of Pont-St.-Esprit stopped eating ergotized bread there were no new cases of ergotism. As pointed out before, the symptoms of many victims lingered for a while and eventually faded away. The strange behavior of many of the nuns of Loudun in 1633 also went away in a similar slow fashion, although some recovered quickly. Each new outbreak of hysteria or strange behavior was interpreted as another act of possession by a demon. At each new manifestation of possession the exorcists would again turn to their task until the victims seemed to be free of the demon or demons.

Most of the major religions, including most Christian sects and Judaism, have more or less official rites of exorcism. In general, the churches tend not to make a big issue of exorcism—that is, if they can help it. The whole business of exorcism is a relic of the Middle Ages and to many church people it is an embarrassment. But from time to time there are events that bring exorcism to everybody's attention. One such event was the movie *The Exorcist*. The film was based on what was claimed to be a true story, about a pre-teen-age child who was allegedly rather violently possessed by a powerful demon. The film was very successful, a record-breaking money-maker.

The film had profound effects that went far beyond its box-office success. Many people who saw the film were very disturbed. Quite a number sought psychiatric treatment. Priests who had never heard of a possession in careers that spanned scores of years were swamped with reports of possession and requests for exorcisms. There was an epidemic of possessions. But no ergot or "germ" caused this epidemic. It was all suggestion, similar to the hysterical suggestion that caused some citizens of Pont-St.-Esprit who had not eaten the tainted bread to show symptoms of ergotism.

In a way, this modern epidemic of possession was similar to those of the Middle Ages. In the Middle Ages, possession was used to explain strange behavior for which there was no other explanation. People knew about demons in the Middle Ages. They were part of life. For a while, *The Exorcist* made demons part of everyday life in the twentieth-century United States. Types of human behavior that had never evoked a single thought of a single demon were now interpreted as possession. Some of the reaction to the film was tragic. There was a rash of incidents involving the killing of people, many of whom were children, because "the Devil had to be driven from them." In most instances, the perpetrators of these do-it-yourself exorcisms had seen *The Exorcist*.

In the film, the possessed child uttered obscenities, urinated on the living-room floor, carried out outrageous acts of sacrilege, and did many other horrible, disgusting things. In time the child did not even look like herself, but had a facial expression that could be described as demonic. This twisting or distortion of the face is called *transmogrification*. It was, and still is, believed to be a sign of demonic possession.

In 1976 a young woman in Germany died while undergoing exorcism rites. The girl, twenty-three-year-old Anneliese Michel of Aschaffenburg, West Germany, had epilepsy. Her condition had been diagnosed, but two priests requested permission to begin an exorcism ritual. The permission was granted by the Bishop of the diocese of Würzburg, and the exorcism rites were carried out with the full knowledge and co-operation of the girl's parents. Exorcism rite prayers were read three times a week in the girl's home. During the rites the young girl refused to eat and she died of starvation.

The two priests and the girl's parents were indicted for manslaughter and brought to trial in 1978. Medical experts testified that Anneliese could have been saved if she had received medical attention as late as one week before her death. The prosecution argued that the priests and the parents knew the girl was dying but failed to seek medical help for her.

The trial resulted in convictions for the two priests and the parents. The defendants received suspended sentences—that is, they did not go to jail.

There have been cases of children behaving the way the young heroine of *The Exorcist* did. There is a rare disease with symptoms that could indeed lead one to believe the victim was possessed. This disease is called Tourette's syndrome. The symptoms are so evocative of *The Exorcist* style of possession that when Dr. Arthur K. Shapiro, a professor of psychiatry at Cornell University Medical College in New York City, published research papers on the disease in 1974, newspaper reporters immediately dubbed the affliction "the *Exorcist* disease."

Tourette's syndrome was first described in 1884 by Gilles de la Tourette, a French physician. The disease generally begins in childhood, usually between the ages of two and fourteen. The first symptoms are tics, or involuntary muscle movements, in the face and elsewhere, frequently in the arms and body. The victim may kick and stamp the feet. Sometimes the patient grimaces, so that it looks as if he or she is making faces, an action that could easily be interpreted as transmogrification. (Some victims of ergotism also exhibit facial grimacing.)

The victims also make involuntary noises. These noises include grunts, shouts, barks, and throat clearing. Another sound made by many of the victims is swearing. Victims blurt out obscene words, four-letter and otherwise. The symptoms can occur singly or in any combination, and come and go. Victims may have prolonged bouts of symptoms. Symptoms can fade and not return for days or months.

The symptoms are so much like descriptions of possession that it might seem that Tourette's syndrome could well have been one of the "blueprints" for the idea of possession in the first place. There are, however, many other human conditions that could qualify for that dubious honor. Our medieval ancestors were not the only ones to have the wrong idea about Tourette's syndrome.

In the Middle Ages, a person with Tourette's syndrome would almost certainly be thought to be possessed. In modern times, victims of the disease were thought to be suffering from various mental diseases such as schizophrenia. They were counseled by psychiatrists who tried to find the underlying causes of the problem through usual psychiatric methods. As it turns out, modern psychiatrists knew little more about the disease than medieval exorcists. Tourette's syndrome is not a mental disease in the usual sense. Although its exact cause is still not known, we do know that some imbalance in the chemistry of the brain brings on the symptoms. It may be hereditary, but there is no strong evidence of this assumption.

Tourette's syndrome can be treated with a drug called haloperidol. Several months are needed for the drug to take effect. However, with use of the drug, sufferers from Tourette's syndrome have been able to lead normal lives. Many of the victims had been treated as outcasts, unable to go to school, keep a job, or take part in normal social activity. But one thing is certain—victims of Tourette's syndrome are not possessed by demons.

Although there is no evidence that epilepsy and Tourette's syndrome are inherited, there is one inherited disease that no doubt accounted for many reports of possession, including one of the most celebrated witch and possession stories of colonial America. The disease is Huntington's chorea. It is a particularly tragic disease for the victim and the victim's family. The symptoms come on slowly. Most victims do not know for sure if they have the disease until they are past thirty. By that time, the victim could have had children and passed it on to them.

The symptoms frequently begin with involuntary movements, a general "peculiar" or "strange" behavior, falling off of intellectual ability, irritability, and fits of anger and temper. There might be bouts of behavior that can be described as silly. The victim may laugh

The Possessed and the Obsessed

loudly for no particular reason. Sometimes victims seem to show remarkable feats of strength, lifting and even throwing heavy objects. They might babble like babies, scream, grunt, or just talk for hours on end. The symptoms come and go. Sometimes the victims can spend months or even years without any symptoms, or the symptoms can continue unabated for months or years. Eventually people with Huntington's chorea deteriorate both mentally and physically to the point where death occurs. There is no cure, although there is some hope of the development of drugs to control the symptoms.

There is very strong evidence that Huntington's chorea was behind the case of Elizabeth Knapp of Groton, Massachusetts, one of the most celebrated instances of possession in the American colonies. Elizabeth Knapp was the daughter of a farmer. As a young girl she was hired out as a maid to the town pastor, Samuel Willard. She lived at the Willard house and, while there, started to exhibit the behavior that led people to believe she was possessed. Samuel Willard kept a careful record of her behavior. He wrote a report on his observations titled "A Brief Account of a Strange and Unusual Providence of God Befallen to Elizabeth Knapp of Groton."

Willard apparently tried to be objective in his report, but he did offer some of his own opinions on the reasons for the girl's behavior.

> This poor and miserable object . . . we observed to carry herself in a strange and unwonted manner. Sometimes she would give sudden shrieks . . . [she]

would burst forth into immoderate and extravagant laughter in such ways as sometimes she fell onto the ground with it.

... upon Monday, October 30, 1671 ... in the evening a little before she went to bed [while] sitting by the fire she cried out, "Oh, my legs!" and clapped her hand on them. ... And forthwith "Oh, I am strangled," and put her hands on her throat.

The next day she was in a strange frame ... sometimes weeping, sometimes laughing and [making] many foolish and apish gestures. ... Afterwards [the same evening] the rest of the family being in bed, she was ... suddenly thrown down into the midst of the floor with violence and taken with a violent fit, whereupon the whole family was raided; and with much ado she was kept out of the fire from destroying herself. After which time she was followed with fits ... in which she was violent in bodily motions, leapings, strainings, and strange agitations, scarce to be held in bounds by the strength of three or four ... violent also in roarings and screamings, representing a dark resemblance of hellish torments and frequently using in these fits diverse words, sometimes crying out "money, money" sometimes "sin and misery" with other words.

Later, according to the Reverend Willard, Elizabeth accused a neighbor of being the cause of her violent fits. Elizabeth claimed that the neighbor or the Devil, who had assumed her neighbor's likeness, came down through the chimney, hit her, and threw her down to

The Possessed and the Obsessed

the floor. The neighbor was summoned to the house. Elizabeth took back her accusation, saying, according to Willard, that Satan had deluded her. This incident may have been the first time Willard began to suspect that diabolical possession was involved in Elizabeth's behavior.

The fits continued, although at times they abated. There were periods when Elizabeth's behavior was completely normal. When it was possible to talk to her, she was asked if she had any idea about what could be causing the seizures. At first she said she didn't know. In time, however, she "confessed" that the Devil had appeared to her and offered her a contract for her soul. In return for her soul the Devil would give her the kinds of things a young girl craved, such as silks, fine clothes, money, "ease from labor," and travel all over the world. Elizabeth's accounts of these visits were vivid. She said that the Devil had shown her a book—written in blood—that contained the names of others who had made contracts with him. Elizabeth went on to say that the Devil had tried to get her to kill her parents, Willard's children, and neighbors.

Elizabeth did not make her "confession" until some time after Willard had suggested that the Devil was at work. The first suggestion of the Devil, as noted before, was probably when the neighbor Elizabeth had accused was vindicated. At the outset Willard and the others had not associated Elizabeth's "distempers" with the Devil. But, as was often the case, the Devil was turned to after all other attempts at explanation had failed. Frequently physicians of the time would shrug their shoulders and declare that the problem was due to possession and there was nothing they could do about it.

It was hoped that Elizabeth's confession would help to make the fits stop, but such was not the case. She had more fits on November 5, and a physician was called in. Apparently this particular physician was not ready to buy the idea of possession at first, and he offered his own diagnosis: ". . . [her] distemper to be natural, arising from the foulness of her stomach and corruptness of her blood, occasioning fumes in her brain and strange fantasies."

The treatment prescribed by the physician was several strong physics, or laxatives. This type of treatment was not uncommon at the time. George Washington was given large doses of calomel, a strong laxative, by the physicians treating him at his last illness. After the strong purge treatment, Elizabeth's fits were fewer and not as violent as before. There was hope that the treatment had worked. The fits, however, did return. The treatments had probably weakened her to the point where she did not have the physical strength to react as violently to the seizures as she had before.

On November 26 she had a particularly violent series of fits.

> . . . she was again seized with violence and extremely seized by her fits that six persons could hardly hold her; but she leaped and skipped about the house perforce roaring and yelling extremely and fetching deadly sighs . . . and looking with a fright-

> ful aspect at the amazement and astonishment of all her beholders. . . . The physician being then again with her, consented that the distemper was diabolical, refused further to administer, advised to extraordinary fasting; whereupon some of God's ministers were sent off. She meanwhile continued extremely tormented . . . she barked like a dog and bleated like a calf.

When she recovered from her fits and had periods of relatively normal behavior, she would tell marvelously detailed stories of her encounters with the Devil. She would tell how the Devil came down the chimney and would sit on her while he tried to persuade her to enter into a contract with him. She also told a story of one time when she was so tired of being pressured by the Devil that she was all ready to sign just so that he would go away and leave her alone. The Devil told her to get a knife so her finger could be cut to get the blood necessary for signing. She went on to say that she could not find a knife, so the pact was not signed. (This tale contradicted other stories in which the Devil could produce whatever he needed right out of the air by simply snapping his fingers.)

A few days later, after Elizabeth had recovered from a series of seizures that lasted several hours, she announced that she had finally done as the Devil told her. She cut her finger to produce blood for the signing. She wove an elaborate story in which the Devil caught the blood in his hand and told her to sign the book. She related how she tried to get out of it by telling the Devil she did not know how to write. The Devil then offered to guide her hand so that she could write out her name.

On later occasions, however, Elizabeth would recant and say her stories of meetings with the Devil and signing books in blood were just stories, and that these incidents were fancies of her imagination.

The most bizarre incident Willard related was one in which a voice appeared to come out of an unconscious Elizabeth, but her mouth did not move. The voice was described as hollow and low, but audible. The voice issued insults and threats such as "you black rogue" and "you had better love me." Similar incidents were related in *The Exorcist*.

Willard took pains in his writings to discuss the possibility that Elizabeth was faking the symptoms, and whether they were due to a natural sickness or diabolical possession. He was apparently quite impressed by the voice issuing from the closed-mouth girl, and that incident, more than any, convinced him that diabolical forces were at work.

Willard, however, resisted attempts to bring Elizabeth to trial for witchcraft, insisting that she needed help and not hanging. The Salem witch trials began some twenty years later (see the later chapter on witchcraft). Critics of these trials used Elizabeth Knapp as an example, pointing out there was no more reason to hang anyone in Salem than there had been to hang Elizabeth Knapp.

Through genetic analyses of Elizabeth Knapp's family, it is almost certain that she had Huntington's chorea. Elizabeth was a member of the family that

The Possessed and the Obsessed 49

originally brought this genetic disease to the United States. In 1630 a fairly large group of immigrants left England for America. Led by John Winthrop, the group consisted of some seven hundred people. Winthrop founded the Massachusetts Bay Colony and was its governor for a number of years. He did not know, as his ship, the *Arbella*, bounced across the Atlantic Ocean, that among the people in his charge were several who carried in their genes what he and many other Puritans would soon see as witchcraft.

Among the people who came to Massachusetts with the Winthrop fleet were three men from the village of Bures St. Mary. It would seem that the citizens of Bures St. Mary were glad to see them go, for they had a long history of outrageous behavior. Two of the men, William and Nicholas Knapp, were related. They soon continued their unsavory ways in America. William was arrested for "public profanity" and selling beer without a license. Nicholas established his record in the New World with even greater dispatch. On the voyage from England many people in the Winthrop group suffered from scurvy, a disease caused by lack of vitamin C. This disease was quite common among people on long sea voyages at the time. Nicholas had sold a fake cure for scurvy to some of his unfortunate fellow voyagers. He was fined five pounds for this offense as soon as the group landed in Massachusetts. Nicholas' wife was hanged for witchcraft in 1653.

William continued to get into trouble. He was fined one hundred pounds for making a speech against Governor Winthrop. Apparently many of the words and expressions William used in the speech were somewhat stronger than those needed to express political disagreement.

There is a record that, in 1653, William's wife owned a licensed "house of entertainment." William died in 1658. One of his daughters moved with her husband to Long Island. Many of their descendants had Huntington's chorea. In 1641 the eldest son of William was arrested for "public distemper." This son later stole the family silver. Another son died at a young age of what was apparently a horrible, but unspecified, disease.

William's third son married Elizabeth Warne, the daughter of "old man Warne," who, among other things, was fined and repeatedly jailed for "neglect of public worship." This son died at about the age of thirty in 1658, the same year as his father. Elizabeth remarried and later returned to Bures St. Mary with her second husband, John Buttery, who, it would seem, was thrown out of Massachusetts.

Elizabeth left behind her daughter, also named Elizabeth. The young girl was hired out to the town minister, Samuel Willard. The younger Elizabeth was, of course, Elizabeth Knapp.

The descendants of the Bures St. Mary group traveled throughout the colonies and carried the Huntington's gene with them. Quite a number of this group, at least ten, are known to have been thought to be possessed or were tried for witchcraft. The symptoms of Huntington's chorea could easily have led people to arrive at a conclusion of witchcraft or possession, particularly in a country filled with people convinced of the existence of these phenomena. Not everyone observed the symptoms of those suspected of being witches with the careful detail of Reverend Willard, who thought Elizabeth Knapp was possessed and not a witch. Most people saw only the obvious symptoms such as weaving motions, grimacing, spasmodic movements, backward and forward jerking of the head, and pursing of the lips as though in pain. Victims of Huntington's chorea suffer a great deal from involuntary jerking of the hands, feet, and legs.

It was widely believed that people with Huntington's chorea, called "magrums" in colonial times, were witches and that the strange jerking movements they made were representations of the suffering of Christ during the crucifixion. Cotton Mather, a fiery colonial preacher who traveled throughout the northern colonies exhorting people to hunt out and kill witches, had a particular hatred for those witches who he said "apishly affected a blasphemous imitation about our Savior."

When witch-hunters stalked the land in Europe and America, no one was really safe from the threat of being accused. People who had mental diseases or conditions such as epilepsy were in particular danger. Undoubtedly many people who were convicted and executed for witchcraft had schizophrenia. They were particularly likely to be suspect since untreated schizophrenics would tend to be "strange" and live on the fringe of society. They might physically attack people or commit other crimes. At other times they would withdraw from reality and babble nonsensically to themselves or others. Epileptics, because of their helplessness during seizures, were more likely to be thought of as being possessed. Schizophrenics, on the other hand, because their strange behavior was a more consistent phenomenon than the occasional seizure of the epileptic, were more likely candidates for the witch court.

While there are no witch trials in our own time and culture, there is still much progress to be made in the diagnosis and treatment of mental illness. Attitudes toward mental illness are certainly more enlightened than was the case a hundred years ago, but here, too, much progress is still to be made. Families of Huntington's chorea victims have, in particular, suffered a great deal from the misunderstanding of neighbors and people in general. And only in recent years has there been a concerted effort to organize an attack on Huntington's chorea, as on many other diseases. Marjorie Guthrie, the widow of the late folk singer Woody Guthrie, and mother of Arlo, has been the major force behind the forming of the Committee to Combat Huntington's Disease. Woody Guthrie had this disease, and his family went through a great deal of suffering, not only from seeing their husband and father slowly deteriorate and die, but also from lack of understanding from others and great difficulty in finding medical help. Woody Guthrie's illness was not immediately diagnosed, and not a few doctors to whom the family went told them that Woody Guthrie's problems came from drinking too much. Many people with Huntington's do become alcoholics, largely out of despair over their condition, but the alcohol they consume is not the cause of their symptoms.

"Whatever possessed him to do that?" is still a phrase frequently heard in our time, and while not everyone who utters it believes that demons and devils can possess people, there are still many people who do so believe.

Vampires, Werewolves, and Such

BLOOD! THE WORD IS SIMPLE ENOUGH, but over the centuries it has generated many complex and intense emotions. To patriots, blood is what is given for one's country. To many, blood is courage. To others, it is awful stuff that can make you faint if you look at it.

To a doctor or physiologist, blood is a suspension of cells in a liquid called plasma. The function of blood is to carry oxygen and other materials to the body cells and to take waste products, such as carbon dioxide, away from the cells. But all that has been known for less than two hundred years. For thousands and thousands of years people knew only that blood was life. The earliest men knew that a hunted animal died when it was hit hard enough to make blood pour out of it. Blood was indeed life: when it left the body, life left the body. Unfortunately, man learned that if a fellow man was hit hard enough to make blood come out, he, too, might lose his life.

Some hunting people today still drink or smear themselves with the blood of animals they have killed. They hope that the blood will impart the strength and vitality of the animal. This was certainly a widespread practice thousands of years ago, and the understandable association of blood with life produced a rich and varied folklore.

It follows that if life and vitality can be gained from taking blood from another animal, these qualities can also be lost along with the blood. The imagination and skill of storytellers soon filled the night with all kinds of horrible things that could suck the blood from people. Among the more widespread of these stories were those that involved vampires.

Vampire stories differ from one part of the world to another, but there is one common thread. All vampires suck blood and must do so in order to exist. Our word *vampire* comes from the Hungarian and, indeed, most of the popularized vampire stories are an amalgam of Hungarian and Rumanian lore. Vampire stories, however, were around long before there were countries called Hungary and Rumania or that most famous vampire region of all, Transylvania, an area in southern Europe that has, at various times in history, belonged to Hungary or Rumania.

Vampires were part of the folklore of ancient Greece and Rome. The Greeks called them *lamiae*. To the Romans, they were *lamiae* or *striges*. They were

One of the roots of the vampire stories was probably the legend of Lamia. Lamia was queen of Libya. Her children were killed in a jealous rage by the Greek goddess Hera. In her grief, Lamia turned into a monster with a woman's head and a body covered with scales. She roamed about sucking the blood of any child she could find. She reproduced herself, and soon there were hundreds of lamias roaming around looking for children to eat.

thought to be evil ghosts that sucked blood. The physical descriptions of these creatures varied with the storyteller. Generally they were thought to be people who had died but were "undead." These undead could return from the grave to suck the blood of the living. In some of the ancient stories, vampires also ate the flesh of their victims.

Ovid and other Roman writers said that vampires could assume the form of birds that flew in the night. These birdlike vampires were usually called striges. Striges were frequently pictured like owls or bats. The writers of that time probably did not know that bats are mammals, not birds. Even if they did know, the distinction was not considered important. Both owls and bats fly and are night creatures, a circumstance that contributed heavily to the dread many people had, and still have, of these animals. The scientific name for the order of birds to which owls belong is Strigiformes (from the Latin *striges*).

Owls have long been a source of fascination. Forty-thousand-year-old drawings of owls have been found in caves. Part of this fascination with owls may stem from their resemblance to people. They stand upright and have eyes in the front of the head, rather than on the sides as do most other birds. Many have tufts of feathers on their heads that look like ears; others appear to have "horns" (actually feathers). They are meat eaters. Some prey on live animals such as rats and rabbits. Others feed on dead animals. They can fly almost silently, and that ability contributed to the idea that they were ghosts or evil spirits.

When an owl strikes at its prey, it throws its wings back and extends its legs. In the strike position, the legs look remarkably like small human legs. It is easy to see how people's imaginations could turn owls into half-human little demons of the night.

The idea that owls are wise is a well-known superstition. The Romans' use of owls to combat the "evil eye" is a lesser-known superstition. The evil eye is a type of curse, usually thought to be given by witches. The evil eye was (and is) believed to be a fairly effective curse that can dry up mothers' milk and cause crop failures and similar misfortunes. People have a morbid fascination with eyes, some to the point of having an eye phobia. A phobia is an unreasonable, often incapacitating, fear of something. A single, large staring eye, or moving eyes in a picture, is a standard feature of many horror movies. The owl's front-facing eyes are large and human-like. The human image is reinforced by the eyes' blinking with upper eyelids.

The ghostly appearance of some species of owls inspired stories about supernatural events related to them. (*Australian News and Information Bureau*)

The voice or hoot of owls is a mournful, scary sound. Some owls have human-like voices. The call of the barn owl is very much like a human scream, so much so that people hearing it for the first time have been known to call the police, thinking that someone is in trouble. Barn owls also have a ghostly, sinister appearance.

Owls are also associated with misfortune. A common folk belief is that the hooting of an owl near a house means someone in the house will soon die. Pliny the Elder (A.D. 23-79), a Roman philosopher, wrote of the owl:

> ... when it appears [it] foretells nothing but evil, and if auspices which import the public weal are being taken at the time is more dreaded than other birds.... whenever it shows itself in cities or at all by daylight it prognosticates dire misfortunes....

The ancient Hebrews also had little love for owls. The following is from the Bible (Leviticus, Chapter 11, verses 13-17).

> And these are they which ye shall have in abomination among fowls; they shall not be eaten ... the eagle ... And the owl, and the night hawk ... And the little owl, and the cormorant, and the great owl...

Bats connote more horror than owls to many people. Many of the drawings of demons in medieval books are based on the faces of bats. There is a rich lore of superstition surrounding these flying mammals. They were thought to be actual demons, or disguised devils. Their grotesque features readily led to stories of bloodsucking and flesh eating.

For almost all bats the charge of bloodsucking, or even so much as biting a person, is undeserved. No species of bat has the slightest interest in eating human flesh. Most are insect eaters. Some are plant eaters. There really is a bat that sucks blood, the vampire bat of Mexico and Central America. Ironically, the spinners of vampire stories in ancient Greece and Rome and Hungary and Rumania never knew of the existence of the vampire bat, the only one in the world that does suck (actually, drinks) blood. Cattle, rather than people, are the vampire bat's usual fare, but the bats will bite and lap up the blood of an occasional human being if nothing else is available. The first Europeans to see vampire bats were Spanish explorers. They observed the bat's blood drinking, a phenomenon that prompted the Spaniards to call the bat *vampiro* (vampire).

Vampires were not always pictured as birdlike things that fly at night. They could also appear in human form: that is, the form of the person they had been before they became undead. The undead legends probably originated in ancient Greece and spread from there to Rome. The Romans carried the stories into the lands they conquered. These stories were, of course, changed and embellished by the local populations. The Romans conquered present-day Rumania. At the time of their conquest, the land was called Dacia. By the second cen-

Vampires, Werewolves, and Such

tury A.D. the Romans had departed, but they left behind their language and many vampire stories, both of which the local inhabitants fashioned to their own liking.

The vampire legends are another example of pagan (Greek and Roman) lore that was incorporated into medieval Christian teachings. The vampire's need for and craving for blood coincided to some degree with the teachings of the early Church. The drinking of

A real vampire bat from Central America. These bats are a problem for cattle ranchers there. The bats bite the cattle and lap up blood from the wounds, which can then become infected. The device on the bat's back is a small radio transmitter placed there by scientists studying the animals. The radio enables the scientists to follow the bat's movements.

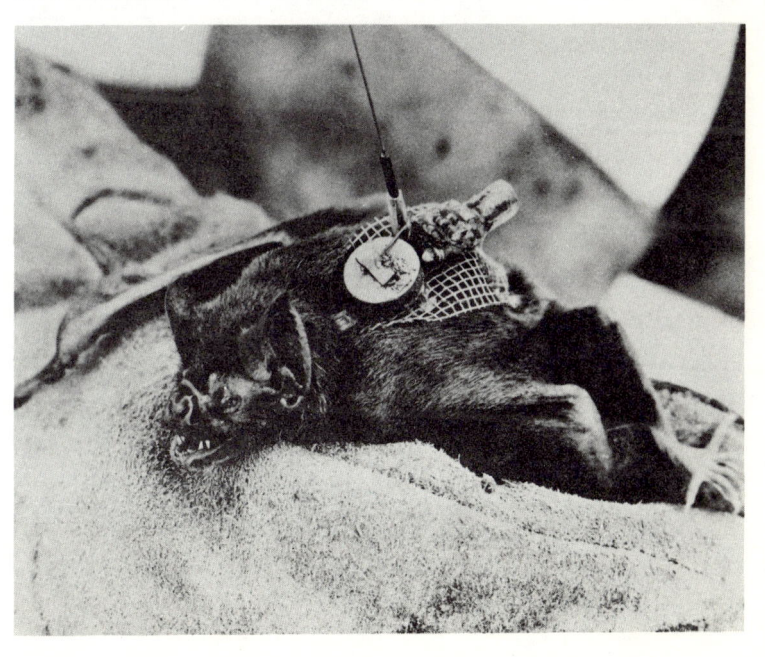

wine at the Mass by the priest is a symbolic drinking of the blood of Christ. In the Gospel According to St. John (Chapter 6, verses 54–56), Jesus says:

> Whoso eateth my flesh, and drinketh my blood, hath eternal life; and I will raise him up at the last day. For my flesh is meat indeed, and my blood is drink indeed. He that eateth my flesh, and drinketh my blood, dwelleth in me. . . .

When Christianity first gained a foothold on the European continent, vampirism was not an official part of church dogma. Indeed, the Church was hard pressed to stop some of the pagan practices that stemmed partially or completely from the belief in vampires. The Saxons, a people who lived in Central Europe but migrated widely, were ritual eaters of human flesh. Passages from the Bible such as the one above seemed to fit right in with what they had always done, and many interpreted such passages from the Bible as church approval of the human flesh-eating ritual. The Holy Roman Emperor Charlemagne (A.D. 742–814) had to issue an edict against the eating of human flesh. He also forbade his subjects to believe that "men and women were *striges* [vampires] who ate human beings." The penalty for violation of this law was death. Another section of the law forbade, also under penalty of death, the burning of people thought to be vampires and also forbade the eating of their flesh.

Church writings from around the eleventh and twelfth centuries indicate that, by that time, vampire

Vampires, Werewolves, and Such

lore had been incorporated into church doctrine. Vampires were widely thought to be the spirits of excommunicated people returned from the grave. Excommunication is the expulsion of a person from the Church. Once excommunicated, the person can no longer receive any of the sacraments of the Church or any other benefits the Church can give. It was believed that excommunicated people could not die completely and were therefore undead, or vampires.

The Spanish artist Francisco Goya, in this plate titled "The Consequences," from the series *The Disasters of War*, showed bloodsucking half-vampires, half-vultures as one of the results of war.

64   *Science and the Supernatural*

Being in an undead state, not quite alive and not quite dead, vampires had to suck the blood of the living in order to maintain themselves. European folklore of the period is filled with stories of ghosts, apparitions and spirits of various descriptions who attacked people and sucked their blood. The usual pattern of these stories is that the ghost who had been excommunicated was recognized as a particular person, sometimes a brother, husband, wife, or other known person, and sometimes some unrelated person from the area. The next event would almost always be the digging up of the grave of the suspected vampire. The unearthing of

In this cartoon, dating from mid-nineteenth-century England, a grave robber is surprised by an "undead" who is rather annoyed at being disturbed.

the grave would reveal an undecayed body, ruddy and healthy-looking from the blood meals it had enjoyed the night before. The body would then be destroyed by the prescribed method in vogue in that particular area.

Modern vampire novels, movies, television plays, and so on, give the impression that there was one and only one way to destroy a vampire. That method, familiar to any watcher of late-night TV, is the driving of a stake through its heart. The stake-through-the-heart method was most widely practiced in Hungary and Rumania. But even there, a nail through the temples was thought by many to be the little extra needed to finish the job. In other parts of Rumania, shoving a piece of garlic in the mouth of the vampire was thought to be sufficient. Also prescribed was taking the heart out and cutting it in two. In Bohemia (part of modern Czechoslovakia) the vampire was buried at a crossroads. It seems, however, with the vampire scares that occurred from time to time in Europe, they must have run out of crossroads. In Ireland, piling stones on the graves was considered to be quite enough. The method employed on the Mediterranean island of Crete was a bit more direct. The head was cut off and boiled in vinegar. Cutting off the head was a widely prescribed way of killing vampires, but different regions had their own intriguing variations on this basic method. In Bavaria a coin had to be placed in the mouth first. In Greece the severed head had to be burned, and in Croatia, part of modern-day Yugoslavia, the head had to be placed between the legs of the vampire. In Serbia (also now part of Yugoslavia)

In this version of a vampire, the creature is shown as definitely human, but with some batlike characteristics.

methods did not extend to so drastic a tactic as decapitation. The Serbs' way, perhaps more genteel, was to cut off the toes of the vampire and drive a nail through its neck.

Burning the entire body, either whole or in pieces like a cut-up frying chicken, was a method widely employed. Macedonians varied the burning method by pouring boiling oil over the body. But some Macedonians maintained that a nail had to be driven into the navel to complete the job. Plants were employed in some parts of Europe. In Bulgaria the vampire had to be chained to its grave with wild roses. In Dalmatia, on the Adriatic coast, the vampire was more or less hypnotized with a bough of hawthorn. And perhaps the most gentle method of all was practiced in Saxony. There the vampire was dispatched by putting a lemon in its mouth. In Spain and Portugal, however, the fear of vampires must have been great. In these countries it was generally believed that there was no way at all to kill a vampire.

Ways to ward off vampires were also quite varied. The holding of a cross to the face of the distressed vampire is, of course, widely known from modern vampire yarns. In Hungary and Rumania, garlic was a staple item in the vampire repellent business. Many of the ways of warding off vampires were pagan practices. In areas that make up present-day Yugoslavia, "living fires" were used to prepare materials used for warding off vampires. The method varied from place to place, but generally a particular kind of wood was specified. The way of lighting the fire was also rather specific. In some areas, the fire had to be started by a young unmarried girl and boy. The pair would strip naked and start the fire by rubbing sticks of wood together. The ashes from the fire were considered to have many miraculous powers, including those of warding off vampires, demons, and witches and protecting possessions such as livestock from evil curses. Various plants, some called wolfsbane, were considered to have vampire-repelling properties. Plants with thorns, such as roses, were widely thought to be anti-vampire. One prescription prevalent in Hungary was the scattering of poppy seeds on roads leading to villages. The vampire, it was believed, had to pick up each one of the seeds and so was delayed. In most areas, however, it was believed that vampires could transport themselves by any number of methods, bodily or nonbodily, so a road block of any description would not stop a vampire. It could go into a house through keyholes, gaps in window sills, chimneys, or any opening, however small.

The aversion of vampires to light was a widespread belief. Fires were kept burning to ward off the vampires and, of course, sunlight was the ultimate anathema. Among the more quaint anti-vampire methods was painting an extra pair of eyes on the forehead of a black dog. This man-made apparition would, it was hoped, scare off the vampire. The demand for black dogs in the area of this belief must have been brisk.

Epidemics of reported vampire attacks swept through Europe at various times. Frequently these epidemics followed periods of upheaval such as conflicts between religious groups, wars, and political turmoil. Although vampire belief spread all over Europe, most of the stories came out of South Central Europe, the areas that make up present-day Hungary, Czechoslovakia, Rumania, southern Poland, and the Balkan countries (Yugoslavia, Albania, Bulgaria, and Greece).

There were religious and political reasons for the richness of vampire lore in this region. It was the scene of contact, and therefore conflict, between the two great divisions of Christianity, the Roman Catholic Church and the Eastern Orthodox Church. The Eastern Orthodox Church had started to split off from the Roman Catholic Church as early as the fourth century A.D. The split occurred more or less along the line of the political division of the Roman Empire into Eastern and Western divisions.

Moslems from the East had conquered most of the Eastern Roman Empire by the end of the fifteenth century, and many of the inhabitants of the region had become Moslems. There was almost constant warfare between Moslems, primarily Turks, and Christians in this region through most of the next two hundred years. In the late 1680s armies of allied Christian countries started to drive the Turks out of much of the area that comprises present-day Hungary and Rumania. The two churches, Roman Catholic and Eastern Orthodox, were then in immediate contention for converts to their faiths. The competition was fierce. Each Church claimed that anyone belonging to the other could not die in a state of grace and was therefore a candidate for becoming an undead vampire upon death. Since each group believed that members of the other were sure to be vampires when they died, the number of vampire reports approached the tens of thousands. In addition to Roman Catholics and Eastern Orthodox Catholics, each of whom were potential vampires to the other, there were Moslems, Jews, heretics of many varieties, and Freemasons, all of whom were potential vampires in the minds of many people.

People lived in terror of vampire attack, for vampires were now no longer a vestige of pagan times long gone but part of widely disseminated church teachings. The churches did not teach that all members of another church were unalterably doomed to become vampires. But many, if not most, of the people tended to believe the worst.

The Church's official explanation for vampires was that they were the spirits of excommunicated people returned from the grave or from purgatory, the place for souls that is between heaven and hell. Indeed, church spokesmen, from time to time, used vampirism as a case in point in discussions of the proof of the existence of purgatory.

The people, drawing on pagan beliefs and their own active imaginations, invented many new ways one could become a vampire. In every modern vampire story, one reads or hears that the bite of a vampire will turn one into a vampire, too. Conceivably, the observation that the bite of a rabid dog would give the victim rabies contributed to this belief. This idea was certainly among the folklore of vampire believers, but it had many variations. The bite or bites had to be received under certain very specific situations, or certain events had to occur afterward in order for the victim to become a vampire. Included among the various ways to become a vampire were being weaned too early, being born with teeth, being born out of wedlock, a witch's spell, being born with a second skin, and being the son of a werewolf.

Ways of telling whether or not a person was a vampire were also quite varied and imaginative. Vampire detection fell into two main categories: detection during the "living" or the nighttime state, and determination of the status of corpses. One of the most widely used materials in the hunt for "living state" vampires was again garlic. Anyone who did not like garlic or seemed to be repelled by its smell was suspect. In many regions there were no methods for detecting walking, breathing vampires. In these areas it was believed that vampires were spirits and as such could not be seen (or, at best, their presence was only barely detectable). In Hungary suspected vampires, including those who were believed to have been bitten by vampires, were tested at trials by having them place fingers on a crucifix or a religious medal. If the fingers turned brown, the individual was a vampire. There were inconsistencies of belief in these proceedings. If a person was indeed a vampire, then he was an undead. Therefore his corporeal presence would imply that his grave was empty, since he was present at the trial. However, many of those presiding over vampire trials did not let such details deter them from burning or otherwise dispatching the suspected vampire. In many places vampire, werewolf, and other legends were combined in various degrees. In some localities *werewolf*, *witch*, and *vampire* were different words for the same thing. In other places there were subtle distinctions.

The most common method of determining the status of a corpse was to dig it up and take a look. Lack of decomposition, as mentioned before, was considered to be an indication of vampire status. Partially decomposed bodies could still be suspect, however. A variety of complicated criteria, again differing from one area to another, were applied to arrive at a vampire or no-vampire decision. In many instances, however, the people took no chances and applied the measures mentioned before to dispatch the vampire. During vampire epidemics, grave openings were so frequent that cemeteries were constantly scenes of grave-unearthing activity.

Also employed were preliminary "grave survey" methods. These techniques were applied to detect vampires in their graves while the graves were still intact, somewhat like a geologist's survey of a potential oil field. In Hungary, one practice involved the use of a horse. A young, unmarried boy rode a black stallion (it had to be completely black) into the cemetery. The specifications for the horse were rather precise. It had to be a stallion that had not yet mated and had never stumbled. If the horse refused to pass over a grave no matter how severely it was whipped, then the grave contained a vampire.

Vampire stories and reports of the nature of the finds in opened graves spread by word of mouth across the countryside. As is often the case, the stories were altered and embellished until it was difficult to separate fact from fancy. Although most of the stories of finding vampires in graves and elsewhere were complete fancies of the imagination, there was a basis to some reports of finding more or less intact bodies in graves, and this basis is more horrible than any fanciful tales of vampires.

There were, unfortunately, instances of people being buried alive. People in extended states of unconsciousness due to epileptic seizures or other conditions may have been presumed dead. There are also various conditions that can produce symptoms of catalepsy. This is a state in which a person is in deep unconsciousness. Breathing and pulse may be so weak as to be almost undetectable. With today's medical techniques, detecting the presence of life in a person in such a state is no great problem. But three hundred years ago, a person in a cataleptic state could easily be mistaken for dead. If a cataleptic person woke up after being buried, he would, of course, try to get out, probably by desperately clawing at the coffin cover. The escape effort had very little chance of success and the unfortunate victim would soon die from lack of air. If the person was suspected of being a vampire, and the grave was subsequently dug up, he would be likely to be found in a lesser state of decay than a person who was in fact dead when buried. The grave openers might find fresh blood in the coffin, the result of cuts and scrapes the victim would get in his desperate attempt to get out of the coffin. The victim would likely not be in the same position as he was when laid in the coffin, which would further lead the grave openers to believe that there lay a vampire who had moved about the night before looking for blood.

Many of the alleged victims of vampires did show symptoms that might indicate they had been relieved of some blood. They were pale, weak, and had signs of anemia. Anemia is any number of conditions that result when there is not enough iron in the blood to transport sufficient oxygen to the cells. The most direct way to get anemia is simply loss of blood. That kind of anemia is temporary, lasting only until the body makes more blood or a transfusion of blood is received. Most causes of anemia, however, are far more complicated than just the loss of blood.

Many types of anemia involve the breaking down of red blood cells, due to a variety of causes. A type that is inherited may have been the basis for many reports of vampire attacks. The disease has a very long name: glucose 6-phosphate dehydrogenase deficiency, or simply G6PD for short. A person with G6PD is usually as healthy as anyone else. But if this person eats certain things, or is subjected to certain types of stress, his red blood cells start to break down and he can get a very bad anemia.

There are many different types of G6PD. One is fairly common in southern Europe, the locale of most of Europe's vampire lore. It is called the Mediterranean type, or favism. The latter name comes from a food called the fava bean. A person with favism will get severe anemia from eating fava beans, and fava beans were and still are a fairly common food in southern Europe.

People suffering from attacks of favism could well have been the basis for many reports of vampire attack. The symptoms can come on gradually, indicating that the victim is receiving a series of nightly visits from the neighborhood vampire. If the victim continues to eat fava beans, the symptoms will get worse and the victim might die from the severe anemia. The severe anemia may produce a wrinkled, wan appearance, and it would not take too much imagination to "find" vampire tooth marks somewhere among the wrinkles. The victim will recover once he stops eating the offending substance, an event that could be interpreted as a cessation of the vampire attacks or a victory over the vampire.

Vampire lore traveled all over Europe, eventually reaching the British Isles. As the stories were told and swapped, they were changed and blended into other local legends. The most famous retelling of the vampire stories is a modern one.

Bram Stoker was an actor and author in turn-of-the-century London. In 1897 he published his novel *Dracula*. The book was an instant success, and the story of Stoker's evil Count Dracula of Transylvania has been retold again and again in films, plays, and books. Stoker

Castle Bran in Transylvania. Dracula's castle was similar to this one. Vlad (Dracula) stayed here frequently as the guest of the Hungarian ruler John Hunyadi. Castle Dracula is in ruins, but it is being restored by the Rumanian government in the hope of making it a tourist attraction.

did, indeed, base much of his book on the vampire lore of Hungary and Rumania, but the main character of the book, Count Dracula, was based on an actual person.

Recent research has shown that Stoker based his Dracula on a prince-warlord of the Transylvania region. But the book was a work of fiction and not an accurate historical account. Stoker wrote his novel to amuse and entertain his audience with a tale of horror. He changed and adapted facts and added his own touches in the same way as thousands of storytellers have, before and after him. However, the historical character on which the Dracula novel is largely based was interesting enough through his own real deeds to deserve some attention.

This person was a prince who probably had the title of Vlad IV. The country he ruled was called Walachia and was part of present-day Rumania. He ruled Walachia from 1456 to 1462 and, later, for a brief period of less than a year, in 1476. He often signed his name "Vlad Dracula," which means "Vlad, the son of Dracul." (The *a* at the end of *Dracula* means "son of.") *Dracul* means "dragon," and his father, Vlad III, was often referred to as "the dragon." The word for "devil" in the Walachian language is similar to *Dracul*, which led many to believe that the prince was called Vlad the Devil.

But the people had another name for the Walachian prince—Vlad Tepes, which means "Vlad the impaler." Vlad dealt with his enemies rather severely, and the name gives a strong idea of just what he did to those

Van deme quaden thyrāne Dracole wyda.

A late-fifteenth-century German woodcut of Dracula.

who displeased him. Vlad Dracula's deeds were indeed cruel and terrible, but they were probably not much more so than those of many of the other petty rulers of the period.

There is little doubt that Vlad Dracula did impale and otherwise cruelly dispatch many of his enemies. However, there is also ample evidence that much of what was said about him was grossly exaggerated. Before and while Dracula was prince of Walachia, he fought the Turks and soon achieved a reputation as a skillful general and a fierce fighter. Many of the people impaled by Dracula were Turkish Moslem soldiers, and Dracula probably resorted to this terrible tactic to instill terror in his enemies. Dracula was praised and honored by a number of Christian leaders for his military success against the Moslems.

Politics during this time was far from genteel. Just who was in power at any given time was usually decided by who could have whom assassinated first. Many of the horrors carried out by Dracula were meant to terrorize his enemies, both Christian and Moslem. He dealt particularly fiercely with a class of noblemen called boyars. Among other things, Dracula believed that some of the boyars had been responsible for murdering his father. So he had several thousand of them impaled, figuring, probably correctly, that the murderers of his father were among them.

In time he made political enemies, probably not because of the terrible things he did but because he interfered with the economic interests of particular groups. In 1462 he was defeated by the Turks and fled from his castle. He was captured and arrested, not by Turks, but by the Christian King of Hungary. Some years earlier, he had sacked the city of Sibiu in Transylvania. Tens of thousands of people were tortured and killed. This act was hard to understand, since the city had given Dracula refuge during another time when he was out of favor in his own land. Apparently some of the people of Sibiu, in particular Germans, got even with Dracula by producing false evidence that he had been a coward and had run from the Turks.

Dracula was lucky that he was not himself impaled or decapitated. Rather, the King let him live under house arrest for some twelve years before allowing him again to be Prince of Walachia, in 1476. That reign was quite short. Less than two months after taking the throne, Dracula was killed in battle against the Turks.

During Dracula's lifetime, some of his enemies printed pamphlets describing some of his awful deeds. But these pamphlets were nothing compared to those that appeared after his death. Printing presses had been invented, and the primitive presses were put to heavy use printing political pamphlets. The intention of the authors of the anti-Dracula pamphlets was to discredit him, and these enemies were not content to let things lie after Dracula died in 1476. The pamphlets, written in German, described his horrible deeds in great detail. One, printed in 1500, described Dracula as a "mad, bloodthirsty berserker." That they were in German is evidence that they were written by Germans in hope of posthumous revenge for the raid on Sibiu.

On the front page of one of the pamphlets is a picture of Dracula lunching at a table set in a field. Dracula is surrounded by thousands of victims impaled on a forest of stakes. And the artist intended to give the impression that Dracula was thoroughly enjoying the disgusting sight. If the authors of the pamphlets hoped to discredit the memory of Vlad Dracula or Vlad Tepes, they did not succeed, at least not entirely. The pamphlets were widely distributed throughout Central Europe, and they were very much in demand. However, the reason for the great demand was apparently not that people were so anxious to take part in discrediting Dracula but that they enjoyed reading the horrible

This woodcut, showing Dracula dining among impaled corpses, appeared on the cover of one of the many sensationalized Dracula pamphlets printed in Germany in the late fifteenth and early sixteenth centuries. The German caption reads: "Here begins a cruel and frightening story about a wild, bloodthirsty man, Dracula the voevod. How he impaled people and roasted them and with their heads boiled them in a kettle and how he skinned people and chopped them to pieces like a cabbage. He also roasted children and made mothers eat their own children. Also many other horrible things are written in this tract. And in which land he ruled."

stories in the pamphlets. They were no different from people today who enjoy reading a horror novel or watching a violent, bloody movie or TV show.

The Dracula story was spread not only by pamphlets, but also by storytellers and wandering balladeers who sang songs of the mighty, wondrous, and horrible deeds

A detail of a portrait of Dracula painted by an unknown artist in the late fifteenth or early sixteenth century. The portrait is in the Castle Ambras near Innsbruck, Austria.

of Vlad Tepes, Vlad the Impaler. In time, Dracula was absorbed into the folklore of Transylvania and the surrounding regions. But in this folklore, Dracula was *not* a vampire. There is nothing in these songs, ballads, stories, and sagas to indicate that any of the people in the region considered Vlad to have been an undead. Bram Stoker, in the novel he wrote in 1897, made Vlad Dracula a vampire, which was, after all, his prerogative, for Stoker never claimed to be anything more than a storyteller.

Soon after Stoker published his novel, the earliest movies were being made. A number of short films on vampires were made in Europe and America in the 1900s, 1910s, and into the 1920s. The first full-length film based, more or less, on Stoker's novel was made in 1922 in Germany. When it was released in the United

Max Schreck as Count Orlock in *Nosferatu*, the 1922 Dracula film.

States in 1929, it was called *Nosferatu*. The title role was played by an actor appropriately named Max Schreck; *Schreck* means "fear" in German.

Most Dracula movie fans would agree that the most famous Dracula film of them all was the first "sound" vampire picture, made in 1931. An American film, it was entitled simply *Dracula* and starred the Hungarian actor Bela Lugosi in the title role. Many people still consider Lugosi the definitive Dracula. The film was based on a Broadway play, which in turn was based on Stoker's novel. Bela Lugosi had also played the lead in the stage play. Lugosi appeared in a number of Dracula films in subsequent years, but real Dracula aficionados maintain that none of these equaled his first effort.

In most of the Dracula films the influence of Stoker is very obvious. The vampire dies at the end through the "only" acceptable method—the stake driven through the heart—frequently after being weakened to the point of death by exposure to sunlight or crosses.

Movies based on the werewolf legends were also turned out by Hollywood during most of the years that Dracula films were in vogue. Some studios made films that featured both werewolf and vampire characters, which is appropriate enough, as these legends were very closely related.

As mentioned earlier, many people made no distinction between werewolves, vampires, and witches. Protestants generally tended to lump all these concepts under the single heading of the Devil's Work. That is, a person could become a werewolf, vampire, witch, or

An advertising poster for Bela Lugosi's first Dracula film.

any combination thereof (depending on where the story was told), through a pact with the Devil.

Stories of werewolves who, like vampires, needed blood to exist go back to the ancient Greeks and beyond. The word *werewolf*, however, is not Greek but probably derives from the Old English word *were*, which means "man," and *wolf*. *Lycanthrope* and *lycanthropy*, more clinical terms for the werewolf and the werewolf phenomenon, do come from the Greek words *lycos*, "wolf," and *anthropos*, "man." Werewolf myths vary, but the basic one is that the werewolf is a man changed into a wolf. In different legends, a person becomes a werewolf through witchcraft, evil spirits such as demons, or simply because he wants to. The need for a full moon to effect the transition from man to wolf is a familiar theme in werewolf movies and was an element in many of these legends. In most of the European werewolf legends, only men could be werewolves. However, women are prominent in Armenian and Ethiopian werewolf stories. In many stories some kind of incantation must be said, and in others an ointment has to rubbed on the skin of the werewolf to bring about the change. The most direct approach was simply putting on a wolfskin. Some werewolf stories involve only a partial change.

In Europe, werewolf "epidemics" usually coincided with periods of witchcraft and/or vampire hysteria. Werewolf stories were particularly prevalent in Russia —understandable in a country that had a fairly large wolf population. Where there were no wolves there were werebears, and weretiger stories are found in Asian mythology.

The wolf has always been a feared animal, but there is very little basis for this fear. The folklore of many peoples is filled with accounts of packs of wolves attacking and devouring people. There have certainly been isolated cases of wolves attacking people. There have also been isolated cases of attacks by dogs, cats, goats, and even chickens, but these isolated cases have not earned for these animals so widespread and intense a fearfulness as has been ascribed to wolves.

Wolves hunt in packs and generally operate by concentrating on a single animal, such as a deer, until the victim is exhausted. The pack then attacks the prey in a frenzy that is not pretty to look at. The fury of an attack by a wolf pack contributed to much of the awe and fear people had of these animals. It is known, however, that wolves usually attack animals weakened through age, illness, or injury. In so doing, they help cull such weakened animals from the herd.

Wolves howl, and the sound of their howling, coming as it usually does in the night, can send chills of horror through anybody. Wolf howling is a wailing, almost human sound. Recent research has indicated that howling is not a message of horror but a wolf's way of having a good time. Wolves have been observed to gather in a circle for what could be described as "community howls." They actually howl at different pitches in what appears to be an attempt to harmonize.

As was the case with vampires, belief in werewolves was quite widespread in eastern Europe, a not surprising circumstance. A fairly prevalent belief was that a werewolf was a human being whose soul could enter a wolf on the night of a full moon. So situated, the soul of the werewolf could satisfy its craving for blood. When the werewolf died it became an undead, or vampire. Reports of werewolves contributed to the vampire scares of the 1600s and 1700s.

Along with witch trials and vampire trials, there were werewolf trials. No one knows exactly how many people were accused of being werewolves, but the figure in all probability exceeded thirty thousand between the years 1600 and 1750. Werewolf trials were particularly unfortunate. While a vampire trial frequently involved a case against a dead person, the accused werewolf was alive, although not necessarily well. Those accused of being werewolves were often sick, pathetic individuals whose strange behavior, brought on by their illness, resulted in the accusation. The frequent result of a vampire trial was the mutilation of a corpse. The sad result of a werewolf trial was the hanging or burning of a person whose only crime was being sick.

The physical descriptions varied from place to place, but certain characteristics, such as horribly pitted skin and fierce-looking red teeth, were fairly common. Marcellus of Sida, a Roman physician (A.D. 117–161) described werewolves as having a yellow complexion, hollow-looking eyes, and a dry tongue. Other points of description of werewolves that recur frequently are a red mouth; numerous sores, pits, and lesions on the skin; hollow, unsteady eyes; and strange behavior.

Although church officials were likely to regard anyone with symptoms such as those described as something evil and a candidate for burning at the stake, quite

In this rather fanciful drawing, a group of werewolves seems to be waiting, somewhat like the customers in front of a British pub, for the proper werewolfing hour to begin.

a number of medieval physicians regarded such people as sick. Many physicians felt that people who showed werewolf symptoms should be treated, rather than killed. Some of the treatments prescribed by medieval physicians, however, make burning at the stake seem a relatively attractive alternative. Bleeding, large doses of violent laxatives, and enemas were among the milder treatments. Among the most drastic was the surgical opening of the abdomen to expose the intestines and other organs so the "foulness" could be washed out of them.

One of the most widely held theories of human ailments in medieval times was one that had first been put forth by the great Greek physician Hippocrates, and later adopted by Arab and medieval European physicians. This was the humoral theory. According to this theory, there were four substances in the human body corresponding, in their characteristics, to what were believed to be the four elements that made up the universe. The four body substances, or humors, were blood, phlegm, black bile, and yellow bile. The four corresponding elements were air, water, earth, and fire. The amount of and the balance of these humors determined the personality and general characteristics of a given human being. An imbalance of the humors resulted in sickness.

Blood corresponded to air, which had the characteristics of being hot and moist. Blood was also hot and moist, and a preponderance of this humor gave a person a rosy-cheeked look and a cheerful, happy temperament. *Sanguine* is another word for this kind of person. Phlegm corresponded to water, which was cold and wet. People with an abundance of this humor tended to be pale and sluggish. *Phlegmatic* is a term still used to describe a slow, easy-going, rather inward person. Black bile, produced by the liver, was thought of as cold and dry, like earth, to which it corresponded. Another word used for the black bile characteristic was *melancholic* (*melan*, "dark"; *cholic*, "bile"). The melancholic was sad and withdrawn and tended to have a shaggy, dark appearance. Yellow bile corresponded to fire and, like fire, was thought of as hot and dry. Produced by the spleen (or so it was thought), it made a red-faced, generally blustery, short-tempered person. This person was called *choleric*. It was thought, however, that if yellow bile was subjected to high heat, such as a fever from within or generally hot conditions from without, it would turn to black bile and the person would become a melancholic. The expression "he got his spleen up," used to describe an angry person, is another legacy of the humoral theory.

Many physicians of the time believed that lycanthropy was a melancholic (black bile) or maniacal (burned yellow bile) condition. The ancient Greeks and medieval physicians regarded melancholia and mania as the two major kinds of mental illness. The maniac was described as noisy, raging, and generally dangerous. The melancholic was withdrawn, quiet, depressed, and suspicious by nature. Melancholy was considered to be a temporary condition, while mania was more or less chronic.

The humoral theory gradually fell into disfavor and became one more interesting chapter in the history of medicine. The descriptions of werewolves suggest strongly that the basis of the werewolf legend was in fact a real disease. The disease is called congenital porphyria. It is not caused by any "germ." It is an inherited disease, which, fortunately, is rather rare. The symptoms of this disease include sensitivity to light. Exposure to light can cause sores to break out on the skin. The sores tend to ulcerate (fester), causing a generally mutilated, scarred appearance. Dark coloring of the skin

A medieval woodcut showing a werewolf, or something like a werewolf, eating quite a few people.

in spots that are sensitive to light may occur, and there may be excessive growth of hair on these light-sensitive spots. The teeth and gums can become red or reddish brown from the deposit of substances called porphyrins. This symptom certainly gave the lycanthrope a bloodthirsty appearance.

There are variations of the disease. In one form called porphyria cutanea tarda, there are many of the symptoms described above. The victim may also be jaundiced: that is, have a yellowish cast to the skin. The victim may also have nervous symptoms such as hysteria and depression. Sometimes the victims behave in a violent way. At other times they are quiet and prefer to be alone. Seizures similar to epilepsy may also occur.

A person with this disease might try to avoid light, knowing what exposure to light will do to him. Because of the disfigurement caused by the disease and the light sensitivity, the victim may be inclined to go out only at night. If the disease itself did not make the person mentally disturbed, then the effects of the disease, such as the disfigurement and the horror and disgust people might show in his presence, would surely tend to do so. The victim would prefer to remove himself from contact with people and could well develop a hatred for people in general, a hatred that could, at times, erupt into violent behavior.

The symptoms of porphyria correspond very closely to descriptions of werewolves. The correspondence is closest between modern descriptions of the disease and those written by Greek and medieval physicians. The correspondence diverges somewhat when we get closer to our own times in the sixteenth, seventeenth, and eighteenth centuries. By that time, over much of Europe superstition and fear had pushed reason and the desire to help out of the way as far as lycanthropy was concerned. This was an ironic state of affairs indeed, for the medieval years were supposed to be a time of superstition and fear while the 1500s to 1700s were the time of the Renaissance, the Age of Reason, and the Age of Enlightenment—movements in human thought that led, among other things, to experimental science and the growth of modern democracy. It was also at this time that insane people were thrown into prisons and left to die. In earlier years, particularly in Spain when that country was controlled by Moslem Moors, mentally ill people were kept in beautiful gardens where they could look at fountains and listen to music.

Vampires, Werewolves, and Such

This German woodcut shows hunters chasing a werewolf down a well. Another unfortunate werewolf is at the left. The caption says that the werewolves ate several children.

Hypertrichosis, an excessive abnormal growth of hair on the face and body, is another physical condition that might have contributed to the werewolf myth. Hypertrichosis is also a rare inherited disease. It could have been a much stronger element in werewolf legends except for the fact that people born with the disease also tend to be born without teeth.

An early well-documented example of hypertrichosis is that of Horatio Gonsalvus. He was born in the Canary Islands in 1556. He was almost completely covered with hair. As a child he was sent to the court of King Henry II of France. At the time, many kings maintained collections of unusal people. Gonsalvus married while in the service of the King. At least two of the children from this marriage had hypertrichosis. Portraits

This woodcut shows the decapitation of Peter Stubb, an accused werewolf.

were painted of Gonsalvus and his daughters. There is an inscription under the portrait of Gonsalvus that reads:

> Portrait of Horatio Gonsalvus for Mercurio Ferrari.
> Here you see Gonsalvus, famous in the Court of Rome,
> On whose human face stood the hair of an animal.
> He lived for you, Ferrari, joined to you in love,
> And here he lives, breathing in death.

There is no evidence that Gonsalvus or his children were thought to be werewolves. However, there is a legend to the effect that Gonsalvus and his family lived in a cave for many years. The cave may have been designed to relieve his homesickness. Many Canary Islanders at the time lived in caves.

A daughter of Horatio Gonsalvus. (*Sketch by Virginia Aylesworth*)

Gonsalvus may not have had the misfortune to have been considered a werewolf, but his portrait does have a strong resemblance to the most famous movie version of a werewolf portrayed by Lon Chaney, Jr., in the 1941 film *The Wolf Man*.

Witchcraft

WITCHCRAFT, OF MANY DIFFERENT VARIETIES, has been practiced in most parts of the world for thousands of years. The exact origins of witchcraft are not known, but everywhere in the world where witchcraft was and is known, witches were considered to be people who had powers above and beyond those of ordinary people. These powers could be used for good or evil, but most witch stories picture the witches as fascinatingly evil people.

As one might expect, most of the witch lore with which we are familiar is European in origin. The Western Hemisphere was settled mostly by Europeans and they, of course, brought their witch lore with them. Black slaves brought African witch stories with them, too, but this lore made little impact on the general picture of witches and witchcraft that most Americans have. One reason for this is that the slaves brought no single body of African witchcraft lore. Slaves were brought here from many different parts of Africa, each of which had its own particular witchcraft. A few of these African witchcraft practices did survive in the New World, particularly in what is called voodoo. Voodoo, however, made much more of an impression in the West Indies than in the parts of North America that became the United States.

Voodoo is an amalgam of African, mostly Ashanti, practice liberally laced with Catholic and Fundamentalist elements the slaves picked up from their owners. Familiar aspects of Afro–West Indies witchcraft are zombies and sticking pins into dolls that represent an enemy. Zombies, somewhat like vampires, are living dead.

A typical voodoo rite involves the drugging and killing of a goat (occasionally a human being). The celebrants drink the blood of the goat and dance themselves into a trance.

Ecstatic dancing is found in many religions, including those of the austere American Shakers and the Hare Krishna people, who can be seen dancing in downtown areas of large cities. Members of the so-called Holy Roller Fundamentalist groups commonly dance themselves into frenzied trances.

In the Western World, witchcraft is generally associated with the Devil. The Christian concept of a witch is that of a person who makes a pact with the Devil. In return for the granting of certain powers and favors, the witch gives her (or his—there have also been male witches) soul to the Devil. However, even in Western culture, witchcraft was not always thought to be the Devil's work. The association of witchcraft and Satan is a Judeo-Christian concept. Witchcraft was probably part of ancient pagan religions and was around for thousands of years before the establishment of Christianity.

In primitive societies, witches, sorcerers, or whatever they may have been called, were thought to have powers that enabled them to communicate with the forces of nature. A man who planted crops needed to have rain at the right time. For a price, the witch could bring rain, or at least make an effort to do so. A witch could also help one get back at an enemy. Again, for a price the witch could cast a curse on the enemy. The curse could be one that would cause death or perhaps one of lesser severity that might cause the cursed person to be unlucky in love or make his cattle die or his crops not grow. On the other hand, the witch could be employed to get someone to love one. Love potions and spells were among the most sought-after services witches had to offer.

One might wonder how witches managed to make a living at their craft, knowing that much of the time their incantations, spells, and so on, would not succeed. It is conceivable that witches could have saved face by offering "money-back guarantees." That is, if the spell, curse, incantation, or whatever failed, the purchaser of the service would not have to pay. In prerevolutionary China, for example, sorceresses who, among other things, claimed the ability to guarantee boy babies were quite common. Male children were considered to be a bonus in China, while girl babies were considered somewhat of a bother. The sorceress would sell some kind of potion for the mother to take, or she would carry out some kind of incantation. Again, the trick here was the money-back guarantee—no charge if the baby was a girl. The sorceress could not help but do rather well, since, in all probability, at least half the births to which she applied her talents would have been male births.

Witches were not always thought to be evil, but it is believed that between the eleventh and the eighteenth century hundreds of thousands of people were accused of being witches and were killed in Europe and America, both by the authorities and by lynch mobs. This killing of people thought to be witches was not a steady thing during this time frame. There were periods of intense witch-hunt activity that usually, but not always, coincided with periods of turmoil such as war and catastrophes such as the Black Death. The Black Death was the bubonic plague that swept through Europe in the fourteenth century. About 20 per cent of the population of Europe died from this cause at that time.

People thought of as witches had been around for a long time before the eleventh century, but while they were sometimes regarded with suspicion and perhaps fear, they were never hunted down and destroyed with such ferocity as they were in Europe in the Middle Ages and afterward.

Witches are mentioned in the Bible. Among the more famous of these was the old hag of Endor whose specialty was raising people from the dead. King Saul of Israel went to her to ask if she could raise the ghost of the dead prophet Samuel, so that he could learn how to defeat a Philistine army that was larger than his own. The biblical passage indicates that, even then, witches were outcasts, for when the disguised King Saul asked the witch of Endor to raise the corpse, the witch replied:

> Behold, thou knowest what Saul hath done, how he hath cut off those that have familiar spirits, and the wizards, out of the land; wherefore then layest thou a snare for my life, to cause me to die?

King Saul had to assure the old witch that he had come to her for her services, and not to trap her in some transgression of the law, before she would apply her skills to raising the dead. The further implication was made that, while witches were outcasts, their services were much sought after, and though the Bible instructed: "Thou shalt not suffer a witch to live," witches were in little danger of being executed or even arrested as long as they did not offend some important person.

The Roman poet Marcus Annaeus Lucanus (Lucan) may have borrowed from the biblical tale of Saul and the witch of Endor in his epic poem *Pharsalia*. In one of the books of this epic he tells how, during a civil war, Sextus, the son of Pompey, went to an old crone called Erichtho in Thessaly. This witch was reputed to have the power to foretell the future through the raising of the dead. In his poem, Lucan tells how Erichtho

An artist's version of the witch of Endor raising the spirit of the prophet Samuel. Note the owl, which is probably the witch's familiar. Familiars were animals, such as cats and owls, which were believed to serve as messengers and general errand runners for the witch.

raised the body of a soldier lying dead on a battlefield. A ghostly voice coming out of the body gave Sextus the military information he desired.

While the witch of Endor and Erichtho the old hag of Thessaly were loners and outcasts, there is evidence that witches, in some places, were organized into groups or cults. The existence or suspicion of the existence of these cults contributed greatly to the hysteria that led to the massive killings of alleged witches. The emerging Christian groups saw witches, who represented pagan practices, as a threat.

The word *witch* itself probably comes from the word *wicce* or *wicca*. A wicca was a priest in one of the groups that the early Christians came to fear. These were a religious group commonly known as druids that flourished in Gaul (now France) and the British Isles before the coming of the Romans and for some time thereafter. Druids were a priestly caste among Celtic tribes.

The druids presided over some marvelously intricate rituals, but they were basically nature worshipers. They danced around trees, were vegetarians, and venerated all things in nature. The druids resisted the Romans in their own quiet way. Open revolt, however, broke out in A.D. 61, when local tribes reacted against the slaughter of druid priests by the Romans. The Romans crushed the revolt, but the druid religion continued, sometimes underground, sometimes in the open, depending on the severity of the Roman rulers at any given time.

The druid religion has had a number of modern revivals. William McAuliffe, shown here, was chief druid in the early twentieth century. This portrait was made in 1911, a time when McAuliffe claimed to be the leader of 300,000 British druids.

Early Christians in the British Isles, mostly more recently arrived Angles and Saxons, who had started to come in great numbers in the late fifth century, were hard pressed to woo the local populace away from their druid practices. The Saxons, who were not converted to Christianity until the very late sixth century and seventh century, then resorted to slandering the druids and their rituals, and in time many of the Celtic religious practices became incorporated into the whole evil picture of witchcraft painted by Christianity.

The early Christians in England preached that the wiccas were murderers who flew through the night and, among other terrible things, ate the flesh of innocent little babies. The people were told that the wiccas could concoct potions that drove people insane. The druids probably did employ plants that had hallucinogenic properties. The use of hallucinogenic plant substances is still a fairly common practice among some religious groups.

One of the Celtic gods was called Cernunnos. He was a bearded figure and had antlers on his head. Cernunnos may have been one of the prototypes of the Devil figure possessed of horns, hoofs, and tail. Pan, the Greek goat god, may have been another Devil prototype. The idea of Satan certainly did not come from European pagans or early European Christians, for that matter. As pointed out earlier, the Satan idea was apparently a Persian one that was later adopted by the Hebrews and modified further by the Christians.

The Celts also knew of Diana, the moon goddess. Diana is a Roman goddess (Artemis in Greek). There is evidence that the Celts were exposed to Greek and Roman ideas long before the Roman conquests of Gaul and Britain, possibly through the Phoenicians, who traveled widely in their trading ships, and possibly directly from Greeks. Diana could transport herself through the air, an ability that the early Christians eventually modified into the picture of the witch traveling through the night air on a stick.

By the early tenth century, church writings included references to evil women who flew through the air to worship the goddess Diana in moonlight ceremonies. These flying women were sometimes referred to as striges—the bloodsucking vampires—in the form of rapacious birds. However, as pointed out in the chapter on vampirism, the strigae concept existed in ancient Greece and possibly even earlier.

The druids did carry out many of their rituals at night. They had particular places, often forest clearings or an area around a sacred tree. To the British and English Christians, recently converted from paganism, these gatherings were the most evil sort of assembly. The meetings were called witches' sabbats, or esbats. The druids did carry out animal sacrifices and they may have indulged in some ritual cannibalism from time to time. Many Saxons, however, especially in eastern Europe, indulged in these same practices even after they had ostensibly become Christians.

Eventually, the druid practices were outlawed. Outlawed or not, the druids or wiccas, now generally called witches, carried out their night rituals anyway. Many people who attended church also took part in witch gatherings whenever they could. Most probably they did so because the witch gatherings or sabbats were fun, and not out of any intentional desire to defy the Church. At the outset, the punishment for taking part in witch rituals was of the order of fasting or short jail terms, but, in time, the rivalry between the Church and witch groups became much more intense and the reaction of the Church to witchcraft became quite se-

A fifteenth-century version of Satan. Many Satans of the period, including this one, still bore a strong resemblance to Cernunnos, a god of the druids. Note the stag antlers. Later versions of Satan portrayed him as the goat god (Pan) or sabbatic god.

vere. Witches reacted in turn by mocking their persecutors. A number of witch groups practiced parodies of church rituals. Among these was the Black Mass. The "priests" of the Black Mass would wear black and were attended by female assistants. They would use a "host" made of the most awful stuff imaginable, and a human skull for a chalice or a chalice carved from wood rather than use one made of precious metal. Black candles made of foul-smelling materials were considered to be essential to the Black Mass.

By the fourteenth century, when the office of the Inquisition had been established, witches were considered to be dangerous enemies of the Church and anyone convicted of witchcraft was sure to be killed, usually by burning at the stake or hanging. The Inquisition was an arm of the Catholic Church. Its function was to seek out and punish heretics—people who did not believe in the doctrines of the true Church. The idea that witches were in league with the Devil was emphasized by the Church. Witches, however, were not alone in this dubious distinction. Other heretic groups were also accused of having made pacts with the Devil. The Protestants also persecuted witches. Indeed, some of the most notorious witch-hunts of all were carried out by authorities in Protestant countries. James VI of Scotland, who became James I of England, was particularly active as a witch-hunter. Both Scotland and England were Protestant countries.

The Inquisition and other instruments of witch persecutions became powerful forces in the lives of people in Europe from the fourteenth to the eighteenth century.

Witchcraft

An accusation of witchcraft was a very effective way to get back at any enemy. All one had to do was accuse someone of being a witch and the authorities would take care of the rest. An accusation of witchcraft was a serious thing indeed. Very few witch trials resulted in acquittals. The threat of accusation and not the activities of witches was the real horror of the belief in witchcraft. Other than the possibility of a person being incapacitated by fear of witchcraft, a witch's spell was incapable of doing harm to anyone, but the burning pyre of wood at the stake was real.

The attempts of the Church to smear witches in fact served to spread the practice of witchcraft. The wild dancing, orgies, and other activities attributed to witches by the Church fascinated quite a number of people, and many actually sought out covens. Ironically, members of covens often escaped prosecution. A member of a coven might well have been a bored aristocrat or some other important person looking for a little action. Candidates for burning at the stake were more likely to be the wrinkled old widow who barely managed to exist in some shack at the edge of the village, or anyone unlucky enough to be accused. Such people probably never took part in sabbats or any other witch activity. Of course, rich and powerful people could also be accused of witchcraft as, indeed, they were by enemies who wanted to get them out of the way. But such people of means could bribe judges and escape with their lives. However, wealthy people were sometimes accused so their property could be confiscated.

In this engraving, a sabbatic goatlike Satan presides over the wild dancing at a witches' sabbat. Note the demons in the circle of dancers—the one in the foreground looks very much like a chicken.

Witches were greatly feared and were credited with having terrible powers to do whatever they might wish to do. Yet when some miserable old hag stood accused in the courtroom, somehow her powers were no longer with her. It would seem that being unable just to fly away from her accusers would in itself be proof of innocence. But the witch-hunters made no such interpretations. Anything the accused witch might say was seen as an attempt to delude her captors. If the accused claimed that her very presence at the trial was proof that she was not a witch, the prosecutors might answer by saying that Satan had temporarily suspended her powers in order to fool the officials of the court. If the accused besought God to help her, the accusers would say that she was actually praying to the Devil.

The word *sabbat* may be an allusion to another group that was persecuted in medieval and modern Europe, the Jews. The word for the Jews' day of rest and religious observance is *shabbat*. In many places the Jews had to worship in secret, which only made them seem more like witches. Jews often took the blame for catastrophes such as the Black Death. A frequent accusation during such periods was that Jews poisoned wells. Witches were accused of similar acts. Like witches, Jews were charged with drinking the blood of children in their rituals. The fact that Jewish religious law specifically forbade the consuming of blood in any form whatsoever (orthodox Jewish prescription calls for meat to be salted in order to draw the blood out before it can be eaten) did not deter the accusers. On the other hand, the word *sabbat* may also come from *Sabazos*, a

Greek word used to describe the drunken orgies of the followers of the god Dionysos (also called Bacchus). Sabazios was a Greek god associated with Dionysos. The French word *s'esbattre*, which means to frolic, may also be the source of *sabbat*.

Whatever the source of the word, the concept of the sabbat was one invented by Christian detractors of witches. That word and others such as *coven* were eagerly adopted by people who practiced witchcraft for fun or profit. A coven was generally defined as a group of twelve witches and a leader, for a total of thirteen. The practices of these covens were a mixture of lore taken from Greek, Roman, and Middle Eastern sources, plus a liberal sprinkling of what Christian critics said they were supposed to do.

Some members of covens may have actually believed they had made a pact with the Devil. In some places, the leader would dress like a devil and take the "pact" of the new member. Ironically enough, the costumes worn by the devil impersonator—gowns, hoofs, black mask, and more—were inventions, not of pagans, but of Christian theologians.

Some covens were made up of people who took what they were doing quite seriously, while others gathered in sabbats merely for the fun of it. Drugs may have contributed to the attitudes many witches had toward these proceedings. For example, witches believed that in order to fly they had to smear some kind of oil or grease on the body. These ointments may have contained drugs such as belladonna that produce a giddy, light-headed feeling that could well be thought of as

Witchcraft

A seventeenth-century engraving of "moonstruck" women. It was widely believed that the moon could induce all kinds of strange behavior in people, including werewolf transformations and witchlike behavior in women.

flying. Mushrooms containing hallucinogenic drugs may also have been used.

A typical sabbat might have started off with a "business meeting." Members would report on supposedly successful spells and other magic. Problems of how to deal with authorities might also be discussed. New members would be initiated. There might also be "marriages" of members. Religious rituals would follow, and these sometimes included sexual orgies. There was eating, drinking, and dancing, usually until dawn, when all went home. Occasionally a "serious" coven might kidnap an unbaptized infant, which they would kill so they could eat its flesh and drink its blood. They did not, as many churchmen claimed, indiscriminately kill any child they could get their hands on. Many coven members initiated their own children into the order.

Other than the occasional killing of an infant or the beating or killing of one of their own number for some transgression, witches did little, if any, harm to the society as a whole. Witch-hunters created far more havoc than those who practiced witchcraft. Indeed, the killing of infants and the drinking of their blood was a practice carried out by some witch groups because the Church said they did such things.

Some people afflicted with mental disease confessed to being witches. Since these people acted in a peculiar way, they would almost always be convicted and put to death. Sometimes there were mass accusations of witchcraft, and whole communities would seem to go mad with the frenzy of accusations and the killing of witches.

Witch baiting soon became a way of life in both Catholic and Protestant Europe. Many books on various aspects of witchcraft were written by people who claimed to be experts on the subject. One of the earliest and most notorious of these was *Malleus Maleficarum (The Hammer of Witches)*. Written in 1486, it was a manual on how to torture witches into confessions.

Here a few representative samples of witches' familiars are pictured. One witch is revealing the names of her imps. Imps were tiny demons who became closely associated with a particular witch. Matthew Hopkins, the Massachusetts "Witch Finder General," takes in the scene.

Jean Bodin wrote a book called *Démonomanie* in 1580. It contained little, if anything, that was new on the subject. It was filled with the usual material on how witches fly, how people turn into werewolves, and quite a bit on demons. What was noteworthy about the book was the preface in which Bodin stated that anyone who criticized his book had to be a witch. Bodin's recommendations on how to deal with witches (in particular, torture) were followed by French courts in witch trials for many years.

Books on witchcraft tended to enjoy brisk sales, especially during periods of massive witch-hunts. The probable reason for the success of witch books was, not that the readers wanted to learn how to righteously ferret out witches, but that they enjoyed reading the detailed accounts of torture and the sexual orgies of the witches.

King James I, the first king of a joined Scotland and England, was obsessed with witchcraft. He believed that a cousin, the Earl of Bothwell, had tried to steal his throne through witchcraft. A very religious man, he really believed in the existence of witches and he felt that one of his most important kingly duties was the finding and punishing of witches. A Protestant, he believed that Catholics were sorcerers. He also wrote a book on witches, *Daemonologie*. Again, the book contained nothing about witches that had not been said before. However, his recommendations on how to deal with witches had profound, long-lasting effects. For he was, after all, the King.

James advocated the death penalty for witches and maintained that evidence from almost any source was

In this engraving, dating from the 1580s, a woman accused and convicted of being a witch is burned at the stake.

valid if it would help to dispatch a witch. Among the types of evidence he deemed acceptable was so-called spectral evidence: that is, evidence that appeared in the form of visions. This type of evidence was acceptable from anyone, including convicted witches.

The admission of spectral evidence in witch trials was responsible for the deaths of thousands of people. For now anyone could condemn a person to death merely by claiming to have had a dream or vision that the accused had performed some kind of witchly act.

Many of James's thoughts on witches were incorporated into the Witchcraft Act passed while he was King. His influence continued for many years after his death both in Europe and in the colonies founded by Englishmen in America. Indeed, one of the most celebrated cases of mass witch hysteria occurred in colonial America, and the admission of spectral evidence was an important factor in this incident.

The Puritans were firm believers in witchcraft and the Devil. When they came to Massachusetts in the early 1600s, they had no reason to believe that the Devil would stay behind in Europe. Quite the contrary —the Devil was very much on the minds of our Puritan forefathers. Many Puritans believed that Indians were the "Devil's people." Furthermore, Puritans regarded themselves as people chosen by God for his work. And the Puritans saw as one of their tasks the subduing of the Devil and his works in the New World.

This obsession with the Devil and witchcraft contributed to the best-known and most tragic episode of

Witchcraft

King James VI of Scotland, later James I of England, taking a look at some women accused of being witches at the North Berwick witch trials of the 1590s. When James became King of England, he brought his zeal for witch-hunting with him.

witch-hunting in American history, the Salem witch trials of the 1690s. While the Puritans' frightened obsession with Satan may have set the stage for the tragedy, ergot—the fungus that commonly infects rye and was the cause of the madness in Pont-St.-Esprit in 1951—may have been the curtain-raiser.

Salem, in 1692, was a small collection of cabins some twenty miles north of Boston. Actually, there were two "Salems," Salem Village and Salem Town. The farms of Salem Village supplied most of the food for Salem Town, some five miles away. What was called Salem Village in 1692 is today called Danvers. The first reports of witches came out of Salem Village. The witch trials took place in Salem Town, still called Salem today. The distinction is important. Salem Village was mostly made up of farms, and the main crop grown on these farms was rye. Rye is as important a grain as wheat in many parts of the world. Real rye bread, for example, is made from rye flour. (The rye bread sold in the United States today, however, is likely to contain more wheat flour than rye flour.)

There was little, if any, wheat grown in Massachusetts Colony in the 1690s. Almost all baked goods were made with rye flour. Wild rye grew in great abundance in Massachusetts when Europeans first settled there. The Puritans, however, regarded the native rye as inferior to their own, so they imported seed stock from England and used the wild rye for cattle feed. They soon abandoned the local rye even for that lowly purpose. They found that it often made the cattle sick.

Not only did the Puritans not know the local rye was infected with ergot, they also did not know that the rye they brought over from England soon became infected by the local plants. So by the 1690s practically all the rye grown around Salem was infected with ergot to some degree.

Just how much ergot was in the rye varied from year to year and was dependent on a number of factors such as amount of rainfall, when the rye was planted, soil conditions, and temperature. The effects of ergot on those who eat it is dependent on how much is taken in, and how fast. The constant intake of ergot can have a severe effect.

The first hint of deviltry in Salem was seen in the strange behavior of a group of young girls, who had formed a friendship circle. They frequently spent the evening together, usually at the home of the parish minister, Samuel Parris. (One of the girls was Parris' daughter. Others in the group were farmers' daughters and house servants.) There was little else for young people to do in Salem at the time. Visiting one another was about the only diversion and entertainment allowed by the stern Puritan way of life.

In late December of 1691 the girls started showing their strange symptoms. They had convulsive fits. They spoke in garbled gibberish. Their bodies twisted in strange ways. At times they screamed. Their faces were twisted and they made gestures that had no apparent meaning.

The Reverend Parris called on the only physician around. All the physician had to offer was the possibility that the girls might be bewitched—that is, some witch or witches had cast a spell on them. Parris could have expected little else from the physician. At the time, "bewitched" was a frequent diagnosis and was generally a euphemism for "I haven't the foggiest idea of what's wrong."

Parris and other ministers then held fasting and prayer meetings. There is evidence that, at first, Parris was not too eager to accept the witchcraft diagnosis.

One of the neighbors, however, took it upon herself to conduct a "test" for witchcraft. This test was the "witch cake," one of the oldest of such divinations.

A witch cake was made of flour and urine from the person thought to be bewitched. The cake was baked and then fed to a dog. If the dog behaved similarly to the afflicted, then it was assumed that the cause of the affliction was witchcraft.

There is no record of what happened to the unfortunate dog. However, since the only flour available with which to make the cake was liberally laced with ergot and since there was probably ergot in the urine of the afflicted girls, it would seem that the dog could have indeed behaved in a rather strange way. It is known that the girls started to make accusations of witchcraft soon after the witch cake was baked.

One of the first to be accused by the girls was Tituba, a house slave owned by Samuel Parris. In fact, it was Tituba who did the actual work of making the witch cake. However, the idea of the cake was the neighbor's and not Tituba's. The neighbor figured that Tituba must have known how to make things like witch cakes. After all, Tituba was dark-skinned and to the Puritans black was associated with the Devil and with witches. The Devil and assorted demons were frequently described as being black men.

The title page of Cotton Mather's *The Wonders of the Invisible World*, in which he described the 1692 Salem witch trials. He also included an account of a "late outrage committed by a knot of Witches in Swede-Land [Sweden]." The Swedish incidents also involved the accusations of children.

The Wonders of the Invisible World:

Being an Account of the

TRYALS

OF

Several Witches,

Lately Exected in

NEW-ENGLAND:

And of several remarkable Curiosities therein Occurring.

Together with,

I. Observations upon the Nature, the Number, and the Operations of the Devils.
II. A short Narrative of a late outrage committed by a knot of Witches in *Swede-Land*, very much resembling, and so far explaining, that under which *New-England* has laboured.
III. Some Councels directing a due Improvement of the Terrible things lately done by the unusual and amazing Range of Evil-Spirits in *New-England*.
IV. A brief Discourse upon those *Temptations* which are the more ordinary Devices of Satan.

By COTTON MATHER.

Published by the Special Command of his EXCELLENCY the Governour of the Province of the *Massachusetts-Bay* in *New-England*.

Printed first, at *Boston* in *New-England*; and Reprinted at *London*, for *John Dunton*, at the *Raven* in the *Poultry*. 1693.

It is widely believed that the girls became obsessed with witchcraft through listening to stories of such things related by Tituba. Most of the accounts of the goings on in Salem lay the blame for the whole business on Tituba. But there is evidence that Tituba was more a victim of the Salem witchcraft mania than its instigator.

After the girls accused Tituba, she was interrogated and urged to confess. Tituba did confess. In all probability she had little choice in the matter. Tituba was from the West Indies. To this day, the West Indies are associated with voodoo and other kinds of magic and witchcraft. The good, pious men of Salem who questioned Tituba may have felt that Tituba just had to be a witch, since she was dark-skinned and from voodoo country. Curiously, however, details of Tituba's confession did not correspond to Afro-West Indies witchcraft lore. Tituba talked freely of witches flying about on broomsticks, conversations with the Devil, sabbats, and black men. All of these were common elements of English witchcraft superstition of that period. Tituba, no doubt, picked up all those witch stories from her Puritan captors.

Although Tituba was falsely accused as a troublemaker, she was much more fortunate than most of the other accused. She was not hanged or otherwise done away with as a consequence of being considered a witch. Before the episode was over, some 234 were accused and jailed. Nineteen were hanged and one man, Giles Corey, was pressed to death with heavy stones in an attempt to get him to confess.

Witchcraft

One artist's version of Tituba telling witch stories to a fascinated group of Salem girls.

It would seem that a whole town had gone mad. If ergot was indeed the cause of Salem's madness, Salem was by no means the first town, or the last, to have had this experience. From time to time, entire towns had gone mad when their bread supply was made from ergotized flour. The incident at Pont-St.-Esprit is the classic case in point. The nature of the planting season before that tragic winter of 1691–92 further suggests that the Devil in Salem was ergot.

Due to the existence of ergot in the native rye, in all probability ergot was always present in the Salem rye crop to some degree. But in most years there was not enough to produce the hallucinations and other symptoms of ergotism. Certain conditions, such as periods of wetness, can increase the growth of ergot. The summer of 1691 was wet and stormy. In the spring of 1691 there had also been more rain than usual, the wet weather continuing into the summer. The rye was planted in the spring and harvested in August. However, the grain was usually stored before it was threshed, typically around Thanksgiving. Ergot is a fairly stable substance and will not lose strength during a few months of storage. Only about half of a given amount of ergot will deteriorate in two years. So it is fairly certain that the 1691 ergot did not lose any of its wallop between August and December of 1691, when the girls' symptoms started. In that time the ergot-infested flour had been threshed, milled, and used to bake bread and other foods.

Rye grown in swampy, low, wet ground is more likely to support an abundant growth of ergot than rye grown on dry land. This circumstance also seems to fit in with the behavior patterns of some of the girls. Some of the wildest, most extreme behavior was shown by Ann Putnam, the twelve-year-old daughter of Thomas Putnam, a farmer. Interestingly enough, Ann's mother also exhibited some peculiar symptoms during the time of the witch-hunt. Historians have offered the theory that the mother was a neurotic, paranoid woman, who disliked everybody and goaded her daughter to accuse people as a way of getting at the people she hated. But it could well have been that the mother and daughter were both affected by ergot.

Putnam's land was in the western part of Salem Village. Most of this land was low-lying and swampy. Putnam grew rye, and much of his rye was sold to other villagers. There were two other girls living in the Putnam household. These two girls were part of the circle and they were both "afflicted."

After the girls started to make accusations, many adults followed suit and started to accuse their neighbors of witchcraft. Thirty of the thirty-two accusers lived in the swampy western section. However, twelve out of the fourteen accused of being witches at the start of the witch-hunt lived in the eastern section. And most of the people who exhibited a degree of sanity and defended the accused lived in the drier, higher eastern section.

There was, however, an important pair of afflicted girls who did not live in the western section. These were the daughter and niece of Samuel Parris, the parson. The parsonage was almost in the exact center of Salem Village. It is fairly well documented that Parris received most of his grain from Putnam. It was common practice to pay ministers a good part of their salary in provisions such as grain. And Putnam was an avid supporter of Parris.

Many citizens were unhappy with Parris. Salem Village had a reputation for the bickering and divisiveness of its inhabitants. A number of ministers before Parris had left in disgust or had been forced out by one fac-

A typical scene during the Salem witch hysteria of 1692. One of the "afflicted" girls lies writhing on the floor. Neighbors accuse a woman of being a witch, and the accused woman swears before the magistrate that she is not a witch.

tion or another. Putnam, as a supporter of Parris, supplied him with most of his grain. As it turned out, most of the supporters of Parris lived in the damp western section, while most of his detractors lived in the drier, relatively ergot-free eastern part of the village.

There were some afflicted girls in the eastern part of Salem Village. But there is evidence that they had access to ergotized grain. One of these girls was Elizabeth

Hubbard, a servant to the physician. The physician had treated Putnam's wife, and it is likely that the doctor was paid, at least partially, with Putnam's ergot-laced grain. Another servant girl, Mary Warren, was also afflicted and probably was under the influence of ergot. However, it is not known just how or where she gained access to enough ergotized baked goods to get ergotism. She worked for a prosperous farmer whose land was relatively high and dry and therefore generally free of ergot. Before the witch mania was over, the farmer and his wife had both been accused of witchcraft and condemned to die. There is some speculation that Mary may have sneaked into the western village at night to see someone, possibly a lover. She may have eaten ergotized bread during these visits.

Soon after the witch cake was fed to the unfortunate dog, Salem Village went into the witchcraft frenzy. The girls had not yet made any mention of witchcraft. Apparently the "revelation" of witchcraft by the witch cake was enough of a suggestion to get the girls going. Parris later stated that the community had gone "to the Devil for help against the Devil."

The proceedings at the trials are, of course, a matter of public record, so much more is known about the trials than about the events that led up to them. However, there is much in the trial testimony that suggests that ergot was at work. Early in the proceedings, the judges agreed to follow the precedent set by James I and accept spectral evidence. For example, if one of the girls cried out that she saw birds flying around the head of an accused person, the officers of the court accepted such "testimony" as evidence against the accused. The visions and hallucinations claimed by the girls were similar to the experiences of people under the influence of LSD, a derivative of ergot. LSD users, or "acid heads," reported that they saw all kinds of hallucinations, some of them terrifying, while they were under the influence of the drug.

Under the influence of LSD, familiar things can assume weird and terrifying shapes, textures, and colors. For example, a chair can become a snarling, charging bear. A picture on the wall can seem to melt and flow out of its frame to fill the room. Of course, the chair is not going to become a bear to the user unless he knows what a bear is, in the first place. The LSD seems to sharpen awareness and to affect certain memory centers in the brain. Similarly, the visions the "afflicted" girls saw in the courtroom were based on witchcraft stories they had heard from their parents and ministers (not necessarily from the wretched Tituba).

The girls frequently cried out that they saw things they described as demons or birds flying about the head of an accused. When an accused "witch," Nehemiah Abbott, was being questioned, Ann Putnam claimed she saw his specter sitting on a roof beam in the courthouse. The girls frequently complained, cried out, screamed, flailed, and kicked when an accused looked at them. They also complained of being bitten, pinched, or both by the "specter" of the accused. Frequently, all of this wailing would stop when the accused person stopped looking at them.

During the Salem witch trials, Ann Putnam screams that she sees birds flying around the head of the accused woman. Such "spectral evidence" was accepted by the court.

If the girls' behavior was due to ergot in rye grown in Salem Village, it would seem that other citizens of Salem would also have eaten the infected grain and shown symptoms of ergotism to some degree. And much of the behavior of Salemites, accused and onlooker alike, would seem to indicate that practically everyone in Salem was under the effect of ergot to some degree in the spring and summer of 1691.

The effect of ergot is cumulative. That is, the more that is eaten, the more heavy the effect is likely to be. Teen-agers tend to eat when they are together, whether the gathering is for a party, doing homework together, or watching a football game on television. Today's fare is likely to be potato chips, pizza, soda pop, and hot dogs. In the Salem of 1691 there was little to snack on other than bread, biscuits, and other baked stuff that would tend to keep. Since the afflicted girls gathered frequently, they could probably have eaten more ergot-infected baked goods than the other villagers.

Although Salem people at large did not act in any way approaching the wild hysteria of the girls, much of their behavior and testimony would seem to indicate that much of the population of Salem was under the influence of ergot to one degree or another or was influenced by general hysteria. In trial testimony, a number of witnesses accused the specters of the alleged witches of choking them, pinching them, and pricking them with pins. One of the most frequent symptoms of ergotism is a creepy, crawling, itching feeling on the skin. This symptom could easily have been interpreted as being pinched and pricked by a witch's specter, especially under the influence of the emotion and fear generated by the witch-hunt. Victims of ergotism can also have tightening of certain muscles involved in swallowing, a sensation that could, under far less dramatic circumstances than the Salem witch trials, be interpreted as choking. Severe vomiting attacks, a symptom of convulsive ergotism, were also experienced by many villagers.

LSD-type hallucinations were also alluded to in trial testimony. One John Louder testified that some sort of black thing came in through the window and took up a position right in front of his face. In his description of the thing, Louder said, "The body of it looked like a monkey, only the feet were like cock's feet, with claws, and the face somewhat more like a man's than a monkey." Louder went on to say that the thing spoke to him.

Another witness reported seeing strange things appearing in his chimney. The things quivered and shook and disappeared, to be replaced by a bright light that also quivered. The man's wife was with him when he claimed to have seen the apparition, but she saw nothing. Quivering things and dancing lights are frequent in the experiences of LSD users. Other witnesses reported the specters of the accused witches sitting on beams of the courthouse as the "real," or corporeal, person was talking in the courtroom. Such testimony on the part of the afflicted girls may have been maliciousness or hysteria. Whatever may have been the case, seeing a ghost-like apparition of someone while talking to that someone is part of many an LSD "trip."

If the victim of ergotism stops eating ergot the symptoms will fade away. In some cases the recovery is fairly rapid, and sometimes the disappearance of the symptoms is so fast as to merit the description of "dramatic." Frequently, however, symptoms may linger, as was demonstrated at Pont-St.-Esprit. Persistent disorientation has plagued some heavy LSD users for months after they stopped. However, the amount of the LSD-like substance in ergot is a fraction of what is contained in straight LSD. So it would seem that the town-wide epidemic of ergotism would fade once the supply of ergoty flour had been consumed. And the events in Salem in the autumn of 1692 seem to bear out this assumption.

The trials were adjourned in mid-September and were scheduled to resume on November 2, 1692. They were never held in the same form again. In May of 1693, Governor Phips ordered that all persons being held on charges of witchcraft be released. In contrast to the spring and summer of 1691, the summer growing season of 1692 had been rather dry. By September the new crop had been harvested and was ready to be threshed as the old ergotized crop was used up. The 1692 crop, however, was smaller than the 1691 crop. Many people who should, by rights, have been working their fields were either in prison or too consumed by the emotion of the witch-hunt to pay much attention to farming.

The fate of many of those convicted at Salem. The hanging shown here, however, was one of the few witch hangings to occur before the Salem trials. The victim was Ann Hibbins of Boston, hanged for witchcraft in 1656.

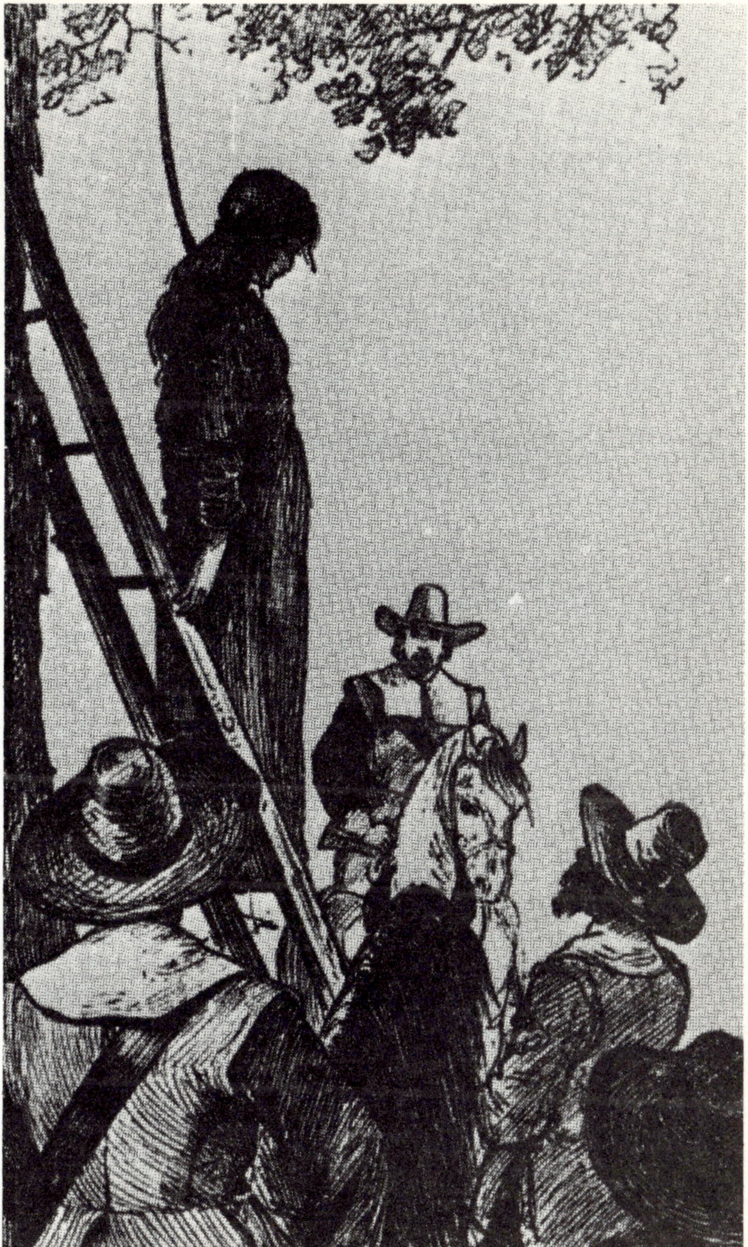

Almost all the judges involved in the trials made public apologies and recantations in the years following the trials. In 1696 Samuel Sewall, one of the judges, issued a statement that included the words "We justly fear we were sadly deluded and mistaken." While the judges presided in Salem they had to eat. And the bread they ate was probably made from ergotized flour. There is a good possibility that the judges were affected by ergot to the point where their ability to judge effectively was impaired.

Even Ann Putman, the most vicious of the accusers, confessed to "delusion." In 1706 she wrote:

> I justly fear I have been instrumental with others, though ignorantly and unwittingly, to bring upon myself and this land the guilt of innocent blood; though what was said or done by me against any person I can truly and uprightly say before God and man, I did it not for any anger, malice or ill will to any person, for I had no such things against one of them but what I did was ignorantly, being deluded of Satan.

Witch-hunts occurred sporadically in Europe during the 1700s, along with the vampire and werewolf scares. By the late 1700s, interest in witch-hunts had faded. The new way of doing things revolved around reason and experimentation. Obsession with witches, vampires, and such became unfashionable as experimental science became fashionable. Science began to grow rapidly in the nineteenth century, and for a time it was widely believed that science and technology could solve all the world's problems. That belief is not nearly so widespread as it once was. Although we, through experimental science, have learned a great deal about ourselves and the world and universe in which we live, war, poverty, and hunger still exist. Indeed, the most horrible weapons of war are the results of the application of knowledge gained through experimental science.

In recent years, the 1960s and 1970s, large numbers of people, particularly young people, seemed to turn away from science as a way to find out more about themselves and their world, to embrace what is generally called the occult. Today's occult is a collection of magic, witchcraft lore, religion, and many other elements, including what are generally called "psychic phenomena." Many people, however, including scientists, believe that psychic phenomena should not be classified as occult. Included in the realm of psychic phenomena are such things as telepathy (thought transfer), psychokinesis (moving objects with "thought power"), precognition (predicting the future), and clairvoyance, which is the ability to see or know about something without the use of the known senses.

Psychic phenomena are being investigated with the methods and techniques of experimental science. While large numbers of scientists continue to dismiss psychic research as nonsense, the supporters of this research can reply that at least scientific methods are being applied in an effort to find out if these phenomena are actual or nonsense.

Believers in witchcraft do not apply scientific methods toward upholding or refuting their beliefs. Neither do practitioners of any other magic. Magic, like science, is a way of trying to find out about things. It is also considered to be a way to make things happen, and science, as we know it, evolved from magic. In the first chapter of this book we discussed the emergence of a class of people called, among other things, shamans. The function of these people was to bring about favorable results in crops, hunting, and other important matters, either by predicting the future or by invoking natural forces, by whatever name, to act in a favorable way. Sometimes the shaman's or witch's work brought about the desired result, probably because over the years the shamans had somehow stumbled onto an effective course of action.

Suppose a farmer of long ago went to a local shaman and asked him or her to make the crops good. After a fee was agreed upon, the shaman might have done a few dances around the farmer's plot, shaking some feathers and animal bones around in the air during the course of the dance. The shaman might then have laboriously put a piece of dead salamander into the ground where each seed had been sown, muttering some secret incantation as he did so. Suppose, further, that one year this farmer or another one could not afford the shaman's fee, but still needed to grow a crop in order to feed his family. The farmer might then have tried a few do-it-yourself methods. The farmer didn't know the incantations and might have been a bit hazy on the dance steps, but he could catch and kill salamanders as well as, if not better than, the shaman could, and he could also get a few feathers and bones to wave around in the air. The farmer was convinced that his

In this drawing by Francisco Goya, many of the common elements of witchcraft—an ugly old crone, a flying broomstick, and an owl—are shown.

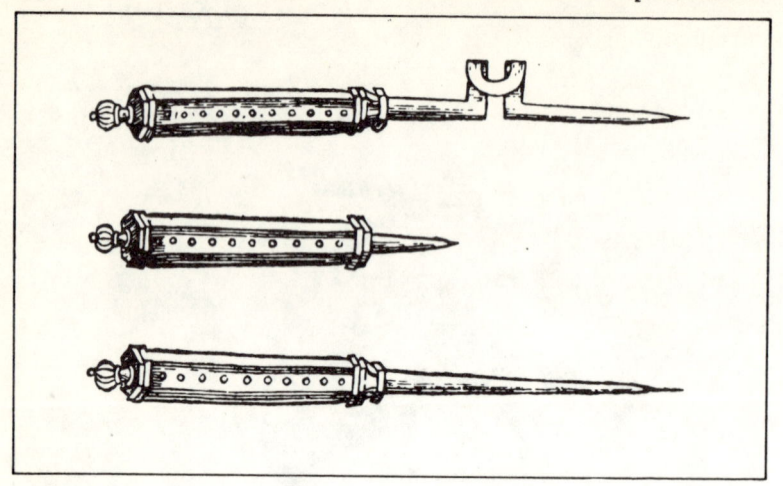

Examples of "prickers" used to search for witches' marks. The two on the bottom are of a type that had a retractable blade that caused no pain and drew no blood, signs often interpreted as proof of being a witch.

efforts would be inferior to those of the shaman and so resigned himself to the prospect of a poor crop. But, he thought to himself, the little bit that I'm doing is better than nothing, so why not give it a try. So he danced as well as he could remember, waved in the air the few bones and feathers he had been able to gather, and carefully put a piece of dead salamander in the ground along with each seed.

Much to the farmer's surprise, that year's crop was as bountiful as any he had grown before. So he thought that whatever he did must have included the right thing to do. Thinking back over what he had done, he remembered that he had not uttered a single incantation, so he surmised that the incantation was not really necessary but everything else seemed to be.

In another planting season, that farmer or another one might have run out of dead salamander before he finished that part of the preparation. The farmer would have discovered that seeds that had been planted with dead salamander had produced many healthy plants, while those without the pieces of salamander had grown into fewer, smaller plants. This observation might have prompted a curious farmer to deliberately plant a few seeds without salamander meat and some with, leaving out all of the other shaman tricks, just to see what would happen. This was science in its infancy, a systematic, deliberate attempt to gain knowledge.

Those who still believe in systems of magic such as astrology and witchcraft are, in many ways, like the shaman and the followers of the shaman. The general idea is that this system has been practiced for thousands of years, so it must be right. Perhaps certain elements of systems of magic such as the pieces of dead salamander might be effective in bringing about the desired result. But a little experimentation will show that a piece of dead fish or compost, or commercial fertilizer, will bring about the same result for a lot less trouble than that involved in catching salamanders.

Are there witches today? There are, without doubt, fairly large numbers of people who like to think of themselves as witches. There are still practicing witches in Africa who make a good living selling their services. Of course, with the continued industrialization and other development of African nations, these witches

This fifteenth-century woodcut shows that some people believed that witches could make some good things happen. This pair is bringing rain. (*Woodcut by Ulrich Molitor*)

will become more and more of a rarity. However, many people in Africa who are good, churchgoing Christians or devout Moslems still seek out witches, from time to time, when the need is so urgent that one needs all the help one can get.

Witches are not to be confused with what are called witch doctors. Witch doctors or medicine men are curers, and much of what they do is not to be sneered at. Many of the materials used by medicine men have therapeutic value, and quite a few have found their way into modern medical practice. Even when medicine men did not give medications, but limited their treatments to chanting and incantation, they were imparting some benefit. Witch doctors and medicine men were among the first psychiatrists. For, if nothing else, they showed that somebody cared, and that alone is often enough to make a sick person feel better.

This sixteenth-century Swiss woodcut shows a curious boy spying on a witches' hut. One witch has emerged from the chimney, another is on her way, while the other two appear to be waiting for clearance for take-off.

There are, indeed, covens today. Covens have always flourished in the British Isles, especially since the antiwitchcraft laws were repealed over a hundred years ago. The number of covens in the United States has increased in recent years as a result of the growth of interest in the occult. These groups are similar to those that flourished in Europe in the 1700s. They are made up of people who need to do something a little out of the ordinary. For the most part, they carry out their activities unmolested by either police or Church, for they are not seen as a threat to anyone. And as long as they do not violate the law, this situation is likely to continue.

Modern-day covens of witches cannot cast death spells or bring up the Devil from hell any more than could their medieval predecessors. So just what do they do? They hold more or less regular meetings in which they carry out various rituals, including, in all probability, the Black Mass. The members pay dues as in any other club. It is highly unlikely that present-day covens kidnap babies to drink their blood and eat their flesh. Even the most avid modern "witch," one who really believes in witchcraft, knows such a horrible act would bring on the full force of the law.

Most coven members belong for the fun of it, and their actions are not harmful to the community. But are there systems of magic, relics of a more superstitious time, that still affect people today? Magic can harm someone only if he or she allows it to do so. For example, if a member of some primitive tribe believes in the effectiveness of witches' spells, and knows that such a spell or curse has been cast on him or her, then that person could well be affected. Such people have been known to die in this knowledge, probably from conditions of stress that brought on heart failure. The person could well be said to have died of fright. Although few people today in an industrial country such as the United States are likely to let themselves be frightened

Witchcraft

A mass witch-hanging in England.

This woodcut shows two witches being burned in company with an accused werewolf.

to death by some spell or curse, many people are affected to a degree by some systems of magic. A system of magic that still has a widespread effect is astrology, the subject of the next chapter.

Written in the Stars?

ASTROLOGY IS EVERYWHERE. You hear and see it wherever you go. Turn on the radio and you are likely to hear some friendly voice waft out of the speaker with words such as "Libra, don't let your emotions get the better of you. Capricorn, attend to financial matters; and as for you, Moon Children, get to that project you've been putting off." Open a newspaper and you will probably find an astrology column. Thousands of newspapers and magazines have such columns. Millions of people in the world believe in astrology and govern much of what they do by what astrologers tell them.

One might think that the followers of astrology are in more or less "primitive" parts of the world. While there are certainly some astrology followers in "primitive" parts, most are in industrialized, sophisticated, "have" nations with advanced technologies and scientific establishments. In the United States alone, millions of dollars are spent every year on astrology and astrological paraphernalia. Actually, astrology is far more likely to have followers in more sophisticated parts of the world. Astrology started among thoughtful people in early civilizations who were curious enough to look up at the stars and wonder what it was all about.

Even prehistoric people must have looked at the sun, moon, and stars. They looked if for no other reason than because they were there. At some point in human history, people began to notice that the sun, moon, and stars appeared and disappeared with regularity, and eventually some learned to predict the movements of the heavenly bodies. Some people along the way figured out that the movements of the sun and moon could be used to measure time. The moon provided an additional measure of time in its monthly waxing and waning. The stars, too, could be used to measure time, but this measurement required more sophisticated observations and techniques that came with the development of civilization.

Markings in Upper Paleolithic caves (forty thousand years ago) that had always been thought to be hunting tallies—that is, a count of how many animals were killed—have been given a new interpretation by some scientists. These scientists propose that, rather than hunting tallies, the marks were a record of lunar timekeeping. The people who made the marks were hunters and not farmers. Since they did not need to keep track of time in order to know when it was the right time to plant crops, to harvest, and so on, it had

Astrology has a long history. These figures were found on the ceiling of the tomb of an Eighteenth Dynasty Egyptian pharaoh. The figure in the middle is the constellation Orion.

been thought they had no need to measure it. Many scientists now believe that, over the years, these people had learned that the animals they hunted had certain habits and patterns of movements that occurred at certain times. This information, which they may have kept track of by marking the waxing and waning of the moon, helped them to hunt food animals successfully. With the later development of agriculture, observing

Written in the Stars?

the moon and other heavenly objects became very important as a way to mark the season when it was best to plant and harvest.

The need to keep track of time has long been important for obvious reasons. It would seem that individuals who became adept at keeping time through observing the movement of the sun, moon, and stars could well have assumed positions of importance and power in their societies. These people could have consolidated and strengthened their power by extending their practice beyond crops to people. To a person in a primitive society, it might seem that a shaman who could look at the sky and tell everybody when was the best time to plant the crops might also be able to tell people when was the best time to do almost anything. So the stellar timekeeper could easily have become the local "fortune-teller."

People have always looked for ways to predict the future. Whoever knows what the future will bring can plot his own life accordingly to take best advantage of future events. Astrology is only one of many systems that have been devised as ways to foretell the future. Astrology, however, is followed and believed in by more people than are other systems. One reason for this large following is that astrology is based on astronomical observations, albeit ancient, and as such has the appearance of being "authentic." Astrology, however, is no more useful for predicting the future or as a system of personal guidance than is reading tea leaves. And, like reading tea leaves, it is a system of magic.

In primitive societies and indeed in many societies

today, magic is much more than pulling rabbits out of hats and making coins disappear. The power of a shaman or witch is based to a large extent on how powerful his or her followers believe this magic to be. Magic was (and is) largely based on omens and signs that are supposed to foretell the future and on other objects of one kind or another that are supposed to make things happen if properly applied.

Much of the magic of foretelling the future is based on the "principle of correspondences." That is, the value of an omen is based on its resemblance to whatever is under consideration. For example, a plant that has heart-shaped flowers would be considered to be effective as a love potion of some kind—if the heart was associated with matters of love, as, indeed, is the case in many cultures.

The principle of correspondences is used a great deal in astrology. One of the signs of the zodiac is Taurus the Bull. A person born under this sign is supposed to have characteristics like a bull—bold, tenacious, courageous. Of course, the fact that the ancients so frequently saw animals in the constellations attests to the importance of animals in their lives. The predictions, personality traits, and other "information" on a person offered by astrologers are all based to a large extent on the principles of correspondences magic, in turn based on the characteristics of the animal or other object seen in a constellation.

One of the enduring arguments among scholars is which came first, astronomy or astrology? That question is not an easy one to answer. For quite some time,

Written in the Stars?

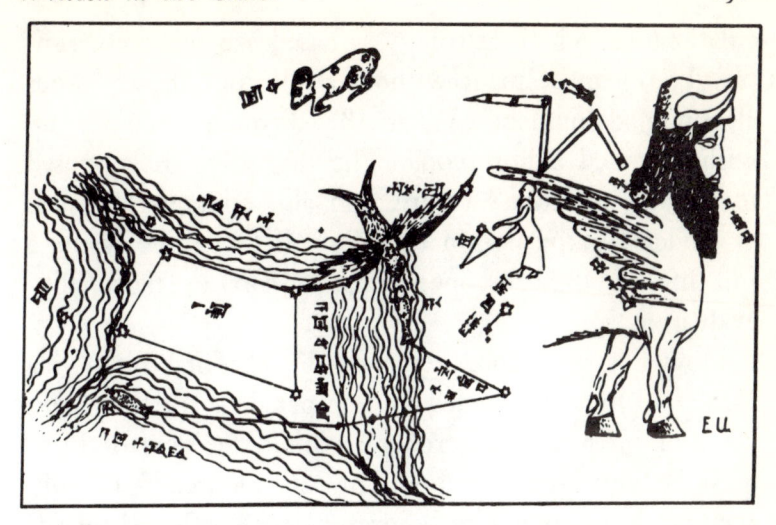

A Babylonian "star chart." The constellation Taurus is shown to the right. The constellation called Triangulum (center) was seen as a plow by the Babylonians. Farther to the left is the Great Square of Pegasus, called I-iku by the Babylonians. I-iku is enclosed by the Rivers of Paradise—the constellation Pisces.

astronomy and astrology meant the same thing, and many of the great astronomers of the past, such as Tycho Brahe (1546–1601), were part-time practicing astrologers. However, it would seem that Brahe, Johannes Kepler, and other astronomers practiced their astrology on the side for the income it brought them. There is a strong body of evidence to indicate that the skills of astronomical observation, such as the ability to plot and predict the apparent movements of the stars, were developed first, and that practitioners of magic later adopted this information for use in a system of magic-astrology. The astronomical observations and calculations on which astrology is based are relatively simple. They can be made without a telescope or any other elaborate equipment. What the astrologer comes up with is called a horoscope. The horoscope is supposed to foretell someone's future, and also contains all kinds of advice for the person to follow if he or she wants a full life. The horoscope is also a sort of personality evaluation.

How is a horoscope determined? The first bit of information that is needed is the person's birthday and place of birth. Some astrologers think the time of birth must be very specific, down to the minute, if a really accurate horoscope is to be drawn up. A celestial meridian is drawn around the person's place of birth. A celestial meridian is a big imaginary circle that is cast over a point on the earth's surface (in this case, a place of birth) and through the north and south celestial poles (the heavens above the north and south poles that is, the north and south horizon), and the zenith (a point directly above the place of birth). In this case, *horizon* is defined as the point ninety degrees from the zenith.

The celestial sphere is an imaginary globe that surrounds the earth in space. The celestial equator corresponds to the earth's equator. The casting of the meridian and the celestial equator divides the celestial sphere into four parts. Circles are then cast passing through north and south points on the horizon as seen from the place of birth. These circles divide the celestial sphere into twelve parts, or houses.

What has been described so far—the first steps in casting a horoscope—is an interesting exercise in basic astronomy that was known to intelligent people over two thousand years ago. As astronomy, it is no less valid now than it was then. But what does all this have to do with any one person's future and personality? The answer to that question, according to all available scientific evidence, is nothing, absolutely nothing. There is more, however, to casting a horoscope. Just how much more depends on the particular kind of astrology one follows.

The original intent of the astronomy described above was not to provide fortunetellers with tools of the trade but to provide a reasonably accurate way to tell time. Observing the waxing and waning of the moon every month was, for example, an easy, handy way to tell time. But as a timekeeper for planting seasons it was inaccurate. The cycle of waxing and waning takes twenty-nine to thirty days, or approximately a month. The word for month in many languages is based on the word for moon.

As a way of keeping track of the days in the month the moon was, and still is, an accurate clock. People soon learned that three waxing-waning cycles were approximately a season, and that twelve of them were almost a year. Ancient calendars, such as the Hebrew, Greek, and Babylonian, were based on the lunar (moon) month. It was the "almost," however, that caused trouble. Lunar months do not divide evenly into solar years (365¼ days), the time it takes for the earth to go around the sun. Twelve lunar months are eleven days too short. Thirteen lunar months are eighteen days too long. The ancient devised a number of ways to

Astrology has been practiced in India for centuries. In this scene from an Indian temple, Saturn is being pulled through the sky on a cart.

handle the moon-sun discrepancy. Some added extra days to months; others added extra months to years. Others had several calendars, each tailored to a particular purpose.

Agriculture was tied to the seasons of the solar year, so farmers had to have an accurate way of determining the time of the seasons. Early farmers found the rising

Written in the Stars?

of constellations was a very good way of keeping track. Keeping track of the rise and fall of the constellations was one of the earliest stellar observations. By the time the ancient Greek civilization was established, following and cataloguing constellations was a well-developed skill.

The Greek astronomer Hipparchus (active circa 130 B.C.; actual birth and death dates not known), was a cataloguer of stars and constellations. With only his eyes and the simplest of measuring aids, he listed and noted the times of rise and fall of about one thousand stars and forty-eight constellations. Twelve of these constellations received special notice because their observed position was such that the sun seemed to pass through them each year in its apparent annual travel through the sky. This path is called the *ecliptic*.

These constellations were, and are:

Aries	the Ram
Taurus	the Bull
Gemini	the Twins
Cancer	the Crab
Leo	the Lion
Virgo	the Virgin
Libra	the Balance
Scorpio	the Scorpion
Sagittarius	the Archer
Capricorn	the Goat
Aquarius	the Water Bearer
Pisces	the Fishes

Many constellations are named after animals, a circumstance that led to the Greeks calling this group of constellations on the ecliptic *Zodiakos Kyklos*, or "Circle of Little Animals." Today they are called the zodiac.

The rise and fall of the constellations in the zodiac gave the early farmer an accurate way to determine the best time to plant and harvest. Lunar months varied, but the farmer could, for example, count on the rise of Libra to show him when it was time to harvest. It was a small mind step to go from the concept of the stars coinciding with the occurrence of events to the concept of the stars causing the events.

In almost all systems of astrology, the cycle begins with the spring equinox, with the sun in Aries, March 21. The starting dates (in most astrology systems) then proceed:

Aries	March 21
Taurus	April 20
Gemini	May 21
Cancer	June 21
Leo	July 23
Virgo	August 23
Libra	September 23
Scorpio	October 23
Sagittarius	November 22
Capricorn	December 22
Aquarius	January 20
Pisces	February 11

Written in the Stars?

While the location of the sun on the person's birth date usually determines the sign, there are other factors that enter the horoscope, sometimes strongly enough in some astrological systems to alter the sign. Among the other important factors in the astrologer's craft are the planets. The ancients called those heavenly bodies that seemed to move among the constellations *planetes asteres* ("wandering stars"). Today they are simply called planets. The ancients knew only the inner five planets, Mercury, Venus, Mars, Jupiter, and Saturn. What about Earth? The ancients did not consider Earth to be a planet, obviously because they could not see the planet they were standing on move across the heavens. They did not regard the sun and moon as planets. The astrologers assigned personality characteristics to the planets, which corresponded to those of the gods bearing the same name.

Mercury	intelligent, fast
Venus	emotional, romantic
Mars	aggressive, courageous
Jupiter	authoritarian, imperious
Saturn	cautious, inhibited

There were three other planets the ancients did not know about, Uranus, Neptune, and Pluto, discovered in 1781, 1846, and 1930. There might be another one beyond Pluto, although evidence for the existence of a tenth planet has yet to be found. Astronomers gave these planets the names of mythological gods. So astrologers assigned to the newly discovered planets personality characteristics associated with these gods.

Uranus	changeable, inventive
Neptune	mysterious, vague
Pluto	powerful, dark

It is certain that astronomers were not grateful for this great power that astrologers arbitrarily bestowed on them. For now, according to astrologers, astronomers had, in effect, influenced the lives and very beings of millions of people merely by assigning names to planets.

According to astrologers, the effects planets have on a person are determined by their positions (that is, the *aspects*) at the time of the subject's birth. If planets are in conjunction (appearing to be close together in the sky), the effects of the planets are strong; whether this is good or bad depends on the qualities that have been assigned to the planets. Planets 60° apart are considered to be strong and favorable: planets 90° apart are strong and unfavorable; planets 120° apart are strong and favorable; while those 180° apart, or in opposition, are considered to be strong and unfavorable.

Another astronomical circumstance considered to be of great significance by astrologers is the ascendant. The ascendant is the sign that is rising on the eastern horizon at the moment of the person's birth. People born at sunrise therefore have a double influence from whatever their sign is, because the sun is in whatever the ascendant is. So a person born in late July at sunrise is a "double Leo." Astrologers expand further on this concept by proposing that the ascendant is associated with the person's "outer character" while the sun sign evokes the person's "inner character." This declaration provides astrologers, and those who want to believe in astrology, with a fudge factor that can be manipulated to suit the astrologer or the receiver of the astrologer's services.

The signs can be divided in a number of ways to provide a variety of interpretations. For example, the signs can be divided into *triplicities*. The signs in each of the groups form "favorable" angles relative to the four elements of Aristotle—air, earth, fire, and water. The qualities of these elements and their humoral equivalents are:

air	energetic (sanguine)
earth	practical (melancholic)
fire	energetic (choleric)
water	emotional (phlegmatic)

Signs can also be divided into *quadriplicities*, based on whether they end in, begin, or merely typify a season through some correspondence. These signs are thought to form unfavorable angles.

Over the years, astrologers have added more and more ingredients until marvelously complex systems were devised that could be manipulated to meet anyone's need. For example, Louis XIV of France, called the Sun King, was born September 5, 1638. That would seem to make him a Virgo, but qualities assigned to Virgo, the virgin, including baseness and poverty, seemed hardly appropriate for a king. But, as is often the case in astrology, there were fudge factors to provide a way out of an embarrassing or undesirable situation. The astrological data proclaimed King Louis XIV an "honorary Leo." Leo is a fire sign ruled by the sun. Leos are bold and energetic, and so Louis became the Sun King. It would seem that the king's astrologers knew well how to keep their jobs and heads.

Not only can astronomers interpret astrological signs, ascendants, and so on, in any number of ways to please clients, but the client can also go to another astrologer if he or she doesn't like what the first one has to say. There are a number of schools of astrology based largely on different ways of dividing up the celestial sphere into houses. The method described at the beginning of the chapter is the basic method from which all the others evolved. It divides the celestial sphere into twelve arcs of 30° each. "Refinements" have been introduced over the years that have complicated the matter and generated bitter disputes among astrologers. One of the points of the dispute is that the twelve constellations of the zodiac are not equal in size as seen from the earth. So some astrologers maintained that the division of the sphere should agree with how much space in the sky the constellation occupied.

A system developed in the seventeenth century by an astrologer called Placidus (the Placidian system) is the most widely used, although a large number of astrologers are returning to the original, equal-house system. But there are at least five or six systems in use, and if one is interested, an astrologer can be found who uses the system of one's choice.

Written in the Stars?

Although the origins of astrology go back to the Babylonians, much of the mechanics that is still practiced by astrologers today was established by stargazers in the Egyptian city of Alexandria some two thousand years ago. Alexandria, named after the conqueror Alexander the Great, became a great center of learning. Among the better known of the scholars who worked there was the astronomer Claudius Ptolemy. Ptolemy linked the signs of the zodiac to the four seasons, thereby "standardizing" astrology to quite an extent among the astrologers of that time. In the Ptolemaic system, the sun entered Aries on the spring equinox—the first day of spring; the sun entered Cancer on the summer solstice—the first day of summer; the sun entered Libra on the fall equinox—the first day of autumn; and the winter solstice—the first day of winter—was the day the sun entered Capricorn.

Ptolemy is perhaps best remembered for his projection of the geocentric universe. That is, Ptolemy saw the earth as the center of the universe and said that everything else in the sky—the sun, moon, planets, and stars—revolved about the earth. This picture of the universe fitted in very nicely with the astrologers' basic premise that the stars and planets controlled the destinies of human beings existing on the surface of the earth.

One would be hard-pressed today to find anyone, other than members of primitive tribes still living a stone-age existence or the most miserably uneducated people, who still believes that the earth is the center of the universe. Yet there are millions of people who

A thirteenth-century Persian astrological commentary. Mars is in Aries (the Ram) and in conjunction with Jupiter. The figures below represent, from left to right, the planets Jupiter, Mars, Venus, Mercury, and Saturn.

stoutly believe in astrology and who will maintain with equal stoutness that anyone who still believes that the sun and planets and stars revolve about the earth is woefully ignorant, stupid, or both. But the geocentric universe was, and still is to a large extent, central to astrology. Modern-day astrologers conveniently alter

Written in the Stars?

their projections and machinations to fit an earth and other planets that revolve about the sun, while still practicing a system of magic based on a geocentric universe.

Another problem with astrology is that two thousand years has passed since Ptolemy "standardized" the system of houses. The position of the stars relative to the horizon—that is, how far above the horizon the star is positioned—is a matter of the tilt of the earth. The earth "wobbles" as it spins. Over two thousand years, the angle of the Earth's tilt has changed so that our view of the heavens has been altered from what it then was. The zodiac has slipped some 30°, an entire house. So if the astrologer tells you you are a "Moon Child" because you were born under the sign of Cancer (June 21 to July 22), you were not really born under the Cancer sign. The sun is in Gemini between those dates. However, such little details do not seem to bother most astrologers, who otherwise pride themselves on the precision of their astrological calculations. A few astrologers want to use the present zodiac. These "sidereal astrologers" are generally held in contempt by classical astrologers.

The discrepancy between the astrological house and the actual astronomical house is but one indication of the differences between astronomy and astrology. Astrology has largely stood still since the time of Ptolemy. Astronomy has grown and continues to grow. When Claudius Ptolemy drew up the system of houses, the existence of the planets Uranus, Neptune, and Pluto was not known. The stars were thought to be much closer than they actually are, and they were thought to revolve about the earth in their own orbit just beyond that of Saturn. The ancient astronomers had not the vaguest idea of how enormously far away the stars really are. Nor did they have any idea of the existence of galaxies, not to mention quasars, pulsars, and so on. Yet astrologers continue to insist that stars—some so far away that it takes light from them, traveling at 186,000 miles a second, up to tens of thousands of years to reach the earth—influence us. The only star that could and indeed does affect us directly is our own star, the sun. Without the sun there would be no life, and probably no planet, for that matter. The moon's gravitational pull and the reflected light from it that hits the earth does have some effect on life. The tides are caused by the gravitational pull of the moon and, to a lesser extent, the sun. The tides in turn influence the life cycles of many kinds of living things, particularly sea life. There is evidence that the phases of the moon may have some effect on human behavior, as well. However, the knowledge that the sun and moon do have profound effects on life on this planet is in no way useful for predicting the future or writing a blanket statement about a person's personality.

What about the stars and planets? The gravitational effect of the planets on the earth and the inhabitants thereof is so weak as to be hardly measurable. There is no evidence whatsoever that the positions of the planets affect life, human or otherwise, on this planet.

The stars have had some profound effects on the history of humankind. People saw they were there, wondered about them, and tried to find out more. This arousal of curiosity, kindled by the stars, contributed greatly to the development of science and the continuing need of human beings to know all there is to know. As such, the stars have had a positive effect on the development of human beings. Astrology, however, has had a negative effect. Tens of thousands of people plan their lives on a two-thousand-year-old system of fortunetelling that has no more value than looking at a crystal ball.

Despite all evidence that astrology is nothing more than another magician's bag of tricks, it continues to grow in popularity. Why does it continue to attract followers in this age of science? For the astrologer, the answer is easy. Astrology can be a very profitable enterprise. As noted earlier, millions of dollars are spent every year on newspaper astrology columns, books, jewelry, and other paraphernalia, and directly to astrologers for personalized horoscopes. Successful writers of horoscopes are quite skilled at writing in a way that will make most people think the words were written just for them. This type of writing and talking has long been the stock in trade of mind readers, fortunetellers, and, of course, astrologers.

While profit is an understandable motivation for astrologers to continue to promote astrology, it is perhaps a bit more difficult to understand why so many people continue to fall for and pay for it. Much of the motivation comes from the need to know the future. To be able to foretell the future has been a strong human desire ever since people knew there was a future to think about. The advantages to be gained from knowing what the future will bring are obvious.

Everyone is faced with the almost daily need to make decisions. Many of these decisions can have significant effects on the course of a person's life. Decisions are not easy to make, and if the decision proves to be the wrong one, the person feels guilty and, of course, responsible for the wrong decision. Astrology provides a way to avoid the responsibility and work of making decisions. Following the astrologer's advice removes the onus from the individual. If the decision turns out to be wrong, one can say it was in the stars and there was nothing that could be done about it.

Astrology appeals to the interest people have in themselves, and it's fun to read something about yourself that supposedly has been written just for you. In recent years, a computerized horoscope service was initiated in Grand Central Terminal in New York City. The customer's birth date was fed into the computer, which gave back a horoscope readout. The venture was very successful and many people gladly paid for the privilege of reading a computer readout that was really no more about themselves than the daily weather report, but seemed to be.

A horoscope is a very personal, egocentric thing. People are, of course, very much concerned with themselves, but there are times when they need the attention and concern of somebody other than themselves. This kind of attention is certainly obtainable from a mate, friend, or parent. But sometimes that may not be quite enough. People may go to psychiatrists or psychologists for the complete attention that they need. But that kind of attention is very expensive. A personal horoscope, personally developed by an astrologer, provides much of the kind of attention a psychiatrist or psychologist has to offer at a fraction of the cost. The astrologer is, in this way, performing a function similar to that of the witch doctor in a primitive society.

A personalized horoscope seems to fill a need for recognition in a world in which anonymity is a way of life. Many people feel they are nothing more than a number in a vast ocean of numbers. The horoscope not only makes the person feel that someone (the astrologer) cares, but also gives the person a tie to the universe, and that alone can make one feel better.

While there are many who will either defend or attack astrology, there is another prevalent attitude, and that is that astrology is a harmless pastime, a little bit of fun that is of no more consequence than watching a Dracula movie or putting a picture of a witch on a broomstick in the window at Halloween. However, of all the supernatural and occult beliefs and practices that are discussed in this book, astrology is taken seriously by more people in the industrialized, developed world than all the others put together.

But is astrology really harmless? The practice of astrology affects everyone in many ways. Even those who don't believe in it are affected. For example, someone born in late July will know that he or she is, according to astrologers, a Leo. Leos are characterized as having

Fire

Air

Water

Earth

A medieval German painting showing the four Aristotelian elements.

strong personalities, determined wills, and the ability to make decisions fast and stick to them. Thus a person may unconsciously assume these characteristics even if not naturally inclined to be that way. If the person is mild-mannered, polite, and generally nonaggressive, he may think, again unconsciously but significantly, that he is a failure because he is not living up to the image of what astrology says he should be.

The characteristics that astrologers assign to people also produce a kind of prejudice. For example, an employer may be deciding on two applicants for a job. He will note from birth dates on the application that one is a Sagittarius and the other is a Libra. Without thinking about it, the employer may lean toward the Libra because of having read somewhere in some astrology column, article, or book that Sagittarius people are often unco-operative and find it difficult to work in a team.

Teachers may form preliminary judgments of their students based on birth dates and astrological signs. Parents may even prejudge their children. Astrological signs frequently enter into conversations when the talk is about other people. Expressions such as "He's a Pisces, and you know how they are" can be as damaging as prejudiced statements based on race or religion.

Astrology is a remnant of an earlier, superstitious age that lingers in what is supposed to be an age of science. Was there, however, some basis for the development of astrology, just as various diseases could have been the basis for belief in werewolves, demonic possession, and witchcraft? Although many astrologers have tried, they have found no plausible natural phenomena to support their claims. Quite the contrary: the application of any of the methods of science to the claims of astrologers can do nothing but reduce these claims to complete nonsense. There are, of course, astrologers who will strongly dispute that last statement.

There have been many attempts to make astrology "scientific." One of the more recent "scientific astrology" movements was based on a concept called *synchronicity*. Proposers of this idea claimed, falsely, that they were supported by the work of the Swiss psychologist Carl G. Jung. Jung had carried out some statistical investigations of astrology in which he tried to find some evidence that people who were happily married had the kind of favorable astrological charts astrologers said they were supposed to have. He could find no supporting evidence for the astrologers' claims. Jung had, however, used the term *synchronicity*, which, at best, can be defined as "meaningful coincidence." Jung was never able to do anything with the concept, in relation either to astrology or to anything else. Some astrologers seized upon the concept as a way of explaining astrological influences. If Mars and Venus are in conjunction on the subject's birth date, this astronomical event will not cause the person to be a strong, aggressive, but loving person; however, the coincidence of the astronomical event will create a strong influence toward that circumstance. There are a number of astrologers who are supporters of this idea, but many have abandoned it. The concept is very vague, even for an astrologer.

Other astrologers embraced the idea of the biological clock. Many plants and animals show a definite rhythm in the way they carry out some life activities. Some plants, for example, have flowers that always open at certain times. Certain species of clams that live in a particular area will "gape," or open their shells, at the same time every day. The gape of the clam seems to be related to the tides, and tides are caused by the gravitational pull of the moon. The knowledge that the heavenly bodies move in a precise, predictable way and that astronomical influences such as tides do have very significant effects on life prompted many astrologers to claim that the discovery of biological clocks proved the existence of astrological influences. That argument is as convoluted and fallacious as any other put forth by astrologers. The tides, for example, do not directly cause the gape of the clams. When these clams were removed from their natural habitat in an eastern coastal area to an aquarium in a laboratory in a midwestern university, the gape occurred at the same time (Eastern Standard Time) that it occurred in the natural habitat. There was no tide in the aquarium.

Biological clocks are internal. They developed through the process of biological evolution. In the case of the clams, those that gaped at a time that more or less corresponded with the tide would be more likely to get food and to survive and reproduce. The descendents of those clams would inherit the tendency to gape at a certain time, tend to survive, and so on. Some animals do respond to the position of the moon, and many seem to be able to adjust their internal clocks to correspond with the tides. Again, this behavior has evolved over millions of years and is not directly caused by astrological influences.

The discovery that the stars and some planets, notably Jupiter, give off radiation that reaches the earth gave hope of scientific redemption to many astrologers. If anything, however, the nature of the radiation that reaches the earth from these sources serves only to weaken the astrologers' case. Radiation from only one heavenly body reaches the earth's surface in sufficient quantity to directly affect it and the life on this planet. That heavenly body is quite obviously the sun. As pointed out before, it is evident that without the sun there would be no one to argue about astrology or anything else. Radiation in the form of moonlight does reach us from the moon. And moonlight could also have some significant effects on human behavior. However, moonlight is but sunlight that has come here by detour, reflected from the surface of the moon. The same can be said for radiation from all the planets except Jupiter, which gives off some radiation of its own.

The radiation we are talking about is electromagnetic. The nature of all electromagnetic radiation is the same. It travels in waves, and the length of the wave makes one kind different from another. Visible light, radio waves, television waves, X rays, radar, and cosmic rays are all electromagnetic radiation. The waves of radar are longer than those of visible light, and light waves are longer than the waves of X rays. Some radiation from the planets does reach the earth. Indeed, some radiation from the stars and even from distant galaxies and the vast space between galaxies reaches the earth, and this radiation does strike people, probably all the time. But there is little, if anything, in that set of facts to give comfort to an astrologer.

The horoscope is based on certain sets of astronomical observations at the moment of birth. It follows, then, that whatever influences the astronomical situation is supposed to have on the newborn have to occur right there and then. When a child is born it receives many times more units of radiation from the fluorescent light tubes in the delivery room than it receives from any heavenly body, including the sun. Objects in the delivery room exert inconceivably more gravitational pull on the newborn baby than any planet. Of course, babies weren't always born in hospitals. Does that bit of history mean that astrologers should turn their attention to plotting the influence of the aspects of delivery room lighting, and the weight and consequently the gravitational influence of the obstetrician performing the delivery, not to mention that of the nurses and the equipment in the room?

Why did astrologers pick the time of birth as the all-important factor? Why not the exact time of conception? It would seem that if radiation would have any effect at all, it would be at conception or even before. Radiation can cause mutations—changes in the genetic make-up of a living thing. But for radiation to cause a mutation, the radiation must strike the chromosomes and, more precisely, a gene on the chromosome within a cell. In order for the mutation to be expressed, it must occur in the gene of a sperm or egg cell that will fertilize or be fertilized respectively, and go through embryonic development and become a new living thing. But time of conception is difficult, if not impossible, to determine in human beings with the accuracy astrologers say is needed to cast a usable horoscope. Biologists did not discover the exact nature of fertilization until the late nineteenth century.

The time of year at which a child is born could possibly have some significant influence on its development. In past times, and in many parts of the world today, certain foods are available or unavailable at particular seasons. The lack of availability of certain foods could have an adverse effect on the health of a pregnant woman and therefore influence the health and possibly even the personality of her unborn child. The same circumstances could affect a young child. Of course, many babies are breast-fed, but what the mother eats or does not eat could affect the composition of the milk. A baby born in warm months would tend to spend more time outside than a child born in cold months. Could the subtle influences of diet and weather have been, to some degree, the basis of astrological personality traits? Such a question is unanswerable without massive research. It would be difficult for someone interested in doing that kind of research to get the necessary funding.

As discussed earlier, psychic phenomena such as clairvoyance do not seem to have any explanation in accepted concepts of physics and biology. For example, a physiologist—a scientist who studies the functions of living things—will state flatly that our sensory organs, such as eyes and ears, can give us information only if certain cells within these organs, called receptors, are stimulated by some kind of energy. In order for psychic phenomena to occur, something must happen that transcends all accepted physical limits of time, energy, and space. And that is a hypothetical set of conditions that many, if not most, scientists are not ready to accept. Yet many people claim, with a sincerity of conviction, that they have experienced many kinds of psychic phenomena in conditions that preclude any stimulation of any receptors by any form of energy.

Parapsychologists—people who study psychic phenomena—have been unable to offer any scientifically plausible explanation for the occurrence of psychic phenomena, but a number of hypotheses, many quite poetic in nature, have been offered. One of these is based on the idea that all life on earth is descended from the same source. That is, at some point in the earth's history, about two billion years ago, life started spontaneously through a biochemical process. Since all life now existing descended from that beginning there is, say many parapsychologists, a psychic bond of some undefined nature between all living things. This psychic bond is, to many parapsychologists, the basis of psychic phenomena.

Astrologers could, and many do, carry the psychic

bond concept a few steps further. There are a number of theories on the origin of the universe. One of the more widely accepted of these is the Big Bang theory. According to this theory, the universe started as a perhaps basketball-size, densely packed mass of matter that was all the matter in the universe. The mass exploded, expanding outward from the original mass. It is still expanding, and all the galaxies, stars, and planets within and the stuff in the vast spaces between the stars and galaxies are the same matter that was in the pre–Big Bang mass of matter. One can then offer a grandly poetic hypothesis that if all matter in the universe is descended from one original pre–Big Bang mass, there just might be a psychic bond of some kind between everything in the universe—living and nonliving.

The chances are extremely remote that any evidence to uphold or refute a hypothesis of a universal psychic bond will ever be found. Even if such a hypothesis is found to be plausible, there would be little, if any, relationship between astrology as presently practiced and this great universal psychic bond. If the bond exists—a sort of *Star Wars* "force"—it would be exerting its influence all the time, not just at the time of the person's birth. And if absolute proof of the existence of this force is ever found, would astrologers use it? If astrologers' reactions to the discovery that the earth is not the center of the universe and that our view of the zodiac constellations is not the same as it was two thousand years ago is any indication, such a revelation would be ignored by most astrologers.

Astrology represents just one more attempt of mankind to find some kind of magic formula that will make life easier and more prosperous with less labor or no labor at all. Similarly, people turned to witches to whom they had assigned superhuman, but evil, powers to get that which could not be obtained through honest labor or because even if they could get what they wanted through honest work, the witch could get it for you without all that hard work. It was always easier to issue a verdict of possessed, witch, vampire, werewolf, and so on, for a sick person and so have a justification for getting that person out of one's life by burning or hanging rather than spending time and labor trying to help him or her. And when hanging and burning fell out of favor, throwing mentally ill people into a jail conveniently called an asylum accomplished the same result.

The world we live in is getting more complicated and difficult to cope with in every passing year. There are many staggering problems, such as overpopulation and the related realities of war and hunger, that must be dealt with if this planet is to continue to be a reasonably decent place on which to live. Mankind can solve these problems only through hard work, both mental and physical. That organized system of work to gain information called science is not the complete answer to our problems. But there is certainly more to be gained from, for example, research to find more efficient food crops than there is from casting horoscopes. Of course we need to look to those human qualities within us that will impel us to apply the findings of scientists for the greater good of mankind rather than for its destruction. But these qualities are not to be found in an astrologer's chart or a witchcraft manual.

Again, it is easier to rely on the astrological prediction of the dawning of the "Age of Aquarius" than it is to do the work needed to bring the time of peace, prosperity, harmony, and understanding that are supposed to be characteristic of this age. There can be no hiding from the realities of the world by embracing ancient systems of magic. Only people, not stars, can bring the Age of Aquarius.

Index

Page numbers in italics refer to illustrations.

Abbott, Nehemiah, 130
African folklore, 97–98
Agriculture, 153–54, 156
Aix-en-Provence, *31*
Alcoholism, 52
Alexander the Great, 161
Angel(s), 17–18
Anges, Jeanne des, *25*, 27
Animal(s), blood of, 55; and demons, 21–22; sacrifices, 106
Armenia, legends, 85
Ascendant (astrological), 158–60
Astrology, 145, *148*, *154*, *162*, 177–78; and astronomical observations, 152–53, 156–57, 164; beginnings of, 146–47, 149–51, 161; birth dates and, 173–74; effect on human development, 165; and geocentric universe, 162–63; and planets, 157–59; popularity of, 166–67; and psychic bond theory, 175–76; schools of, 160–61; "scientific" basis of, 167, 169–74; yearly cycles, 165
Astronomy, 149, 150–51; ancient, 152–55, 158, 163–64

Bat(s), as demons, 59; and vampire legends, 56, 59–60
Bible, 59; and witches, 100–1
Biological clock(s), 171–72
Black Death, 100, 111
Black Mass, 108
Blood, 54, 89; and vampires, 55, 64–65, 73; and witchcraft, 111, 114
Bodin, Jean, 116
Bothwell, Earl of, 116
Brahe, Tycho, 151

Bulgaria, legends, 66
Burial, live, 72–73
Buttery, John, 50

Caesar, Julius, 15
Calendars, ancient, 153
Cannibalism, 62, 106
Castle Dracula, 75
Catalepsy, 72–73
Celestial sphere, 152, 160
Celtic religion, 105–6
Cernunnos, 105, *107*
Chaney, Lon, Jr., 96
Charlemagne, 62
China, sorcerers in, 99–100
Christian religion, 8, 78; and converts, 69; and demons, 18, 21; exorcism, 38; and Satan, 19; and vampires, 61–63, 69–71; and warfare with Moslems, 68–69; and witchcraft, 98–99
Clairvoyance, 137, 175
Constellation(s), *148*, *151*, 155–56
Corey, Giles, 124
Coven(s), 109, 112
Crete, and vampire legends, 65
Cross(es), and vampires, 67
Crossroad(s), and vampires, 65
Curse(s), 57
Czechoslovakia, legends, 65

Demon(s), 10, 18, 19–20, *20*, *26*, 41, 42, *110*, *115*, 116; in animal forms, 21–22; possession by, 11, 22–24, 39; tales about, 8, 9, 59–60; and werewolves, 85
Devil, the, *17*, *110*; black skin and, 122; and contracts for "soul," 44–45, 47–48; origin of idea, 16–19, 105, 144; pacts with, 84–85, 98, 108, 112; possession by, 16, 24, 27, 28, 39;

Puritans and, 118, 119, 122; and witchcraft, 108, 111, 124, 128
Dracula, 74–76, 83
Dracula, Count, 74, 76
Dracula, Vlad, 75, 76–82, *77*, *80*, *81*, *84*; films of, 82–83
Druid(s), 103, *104*, 105

Ecliptic, the, 155, 156
Endor, witch of, 100–1, *102*
Epilepsy, 42, 91; and possession, 15, 23, 29, 39, 51–52; seizures, 12–14; treatment of victims, 14–15
Equinox, spring, 156, 161
Ergot, 27–30, 38, 120, 122, 126, 130, 132, 134–35. *See also* Rye flour.
Ergotism, 126; convulsive, 28–30, 37; epidemics, 28, 31; and witchcraft, 132–35
Erichtho, legends, 101, 103
Ethiopia, legends, 85
Evil eye, 57
Excommunication, 63, 64, 69
Exorcism, 23, *23*, 24, *28*, 30, 38; modern cases of, 39–40
Exorcist, The, 38–40, 48

Favism, 74
Fire(s), anti-vampire, 67
Folklore, 8; vampire, 55–56, 70–72, 74–75, 81; werewolf, 83–86; witchcraft, 97–98
Fortune-telling, 149, 152

Garlic, and vampires, 10, 65, 67, 70
Gaufridi, Louis, 31
Ghost(s), 64
God(s), traits, 105–6, 112, 157–58
Gonsalvus, Horatio, 93–94, *95*, 96

Index

Grandier, Urbain, 24, *26*, *28*, 30
Grave(s), *64*; bodies in, 72–73; and vampires, 64–65, 69, 71–72
Greece, ancient, 19, 55, 60, 85, 106, 155
Greece, modern, 65
G6PD disease (glucose 6-phosphate dehydrogenase deficiency), 73–74
Guthrie, Woody, 52

Hair, and werewolf legends, 83
Hallucination(s), 29, 33–36
Hallucinogens, ergot-produced, 126, 130, 133; and witchcraft, 105, 112–113
Hebrew religion, and the Devil, 16–17, 19; and exorcism, 38; and witchcraft, 100–1, 111
Heredity, and possession, 48–50
Hibbins, Ann, 134
Hipparchus, 155
Hippocrates, 89
Hopkins, Matthew, 115
Horoscope(s), computerized, 166; effects of, 167; making, 152–53, 157, 173–74
Houses, astrological, 163
Hubbard, Elizabeth, 128–29
Humors (of the body), 89–90
Hungary, legends, 55, 65, 67, 70–72, 76, 78
Huntington's chorea, 42–52
Hypertrichosis, 93–94, 96

Imp(s), *115*
Indian(s) (American), and the Devil, 119
Inquisition, the, 9, 108–9
Ireland, legends, 65

James I (England and Scotland), 108, 116–18, *119*, 129
Jaundice, 81

Kepler, Johannes, 151
Knapp, Elizabeth, 43–49, 51
Knapp, Nicholas, 49, 50
Knapp, William, 49

Lamia, 56
Lamiae, 55
Legends, 1–11. *See also* Folklore
Life, origins of, 175–76
Light, sensitivity to, 90–91
Loudun (France), and possession, 24, 27, 29, 30–31, 38
Louis XIV (France), 159–60
LSD, 29; from ergot, 130, 133–34
Lugosi, Bela, 83, *84*
Lycanthropy. *See* Werewolf

McAuliffe, William, 104
Macedonia, ancient, legends, 66
Magic, systems of, 137–38, 141, 144–45; astrology as, 149–51
Marcellus of Sida, 87
Marcus Annaeus Lucanus, 101
Mather, Cotton, 51, *122*
Medicine, 88–90, 92
Melancholic personality, 89–90
Mental illness, 92
Michel, Anneliese, 39–40
Middle Ages, 15–17, 19, 37, 39, 41; medicine for "werewolves," 88–90; witch hunts during, 100
Mohammed, 14
Moon, in astrology, 157, 164, 171; time-keeping, 147, 149, 153, 156; in werewolf legends, 15, *113*
Moslem religion, 68–69, 77–78

Mutation(s), 173–74

Nosferatu, 82, 83

Omen(s), 150
Ovid, 56
Owl(s), 57, *58*, 59

Parris, Samuel, 121–22, 127–30
Persian religion, 16, 18–19
Pharaoh(s), 14
Pharsalia, 101
Phipps, William, 134
Phobia(s), 57
Placidus, 160
Planet(s), and astrology, 157–58, 161, 173; effects of, on human life, 164, 172
Plasma, 54
Pliny the Elder, 59
Pont-St.-Esprit, 32–39, 119
Porphyria, congenital, 90–92
Porphyria cutanea tarda, 91
Possession, 11, 12, 14–15, *28*, *31*, 53; epidemics of, 24, 29, 32, 37–39; ergot and, 27–30; Huntington's chorea, 42–46; and Tourette's syndrome, 40–42
Principle of correspondences, 150
Psychiatry, 41–42
Psychic blond theory, 175–76
Psychic bond theory, 175–76
Ptolemy, Claudius, 161, 163
Puche, Joseph, 35
Purgatory, and vampires, 69
Puritan(s), and witchcraft, 118, 120–24
Putnam, Ann, 126, *131*, 136

Rabies, 70
Radiation, electromagnetic, 172–73
Religion, 14, 18, 21, 98; and the Devil, 16–19; exorcism, 38; and spread of vampire legend, 68–69; and witchcraft, 103, 105–9, 111–13. *See also* Persian, Hebrew, etc.
Rome, ancient, 55–56, 60, 105–6
Rose(s), in vampire lore, 66–67
Rumania, legends, 55, 65, 67, 76
Russia, werewolf stories in, 85
Rye flour, and ergot, 27, 30, 32, 36–38, 119–21, 125–29, 136

Sabbat(s), 106–7, *110*, 111–12, 124
St. Anthony's fire, 28
Salem witch trials, 48, 120–22, *122*, 124–35, *128*, *131*, 134
Satan, *107. See also* Devil, the
Saul, King of Israel, 101
Saxon people, 62, 66, 105, 106
Schizophrenia, 41; and witchcraft, 51–52
Schreck, Max, *82*, 83
Sewall, Samuel, 136
Sextus, 101, 103
Shaker(s), 98
Shaman(s), 138, 141, 149, 150. *See also* Storyteller.
Sign(s), astrological, 158–60
Sorcerer(s), 6, 9, 19, 99, 116. *See also* Witches.
Spain and Portugal, legends, 66
Star(s), and astrology, 148, 150, *151*, 161, 164–65, 172
Star Wars, 176
Stoker, Bram, 74, 76, 82, 83
Storyteller(s), 1–9, 19, 29–30, 35, 72, 76, 80–81; importance to early cultures, 4–5; as priest, 7–8

Index

Striges, 55–56, 62, 106
Stubb, Peter, *94*
Sun, and astrology, 147, 154, 157, 164; and radiation, 172–73
Sunlight, anti-vampire, 68
Synchronicity, 170

Telepathy, 137
Tide(s), and human behavior, 171
Time-keeping, 148–49, 153
Tituba, 122, 124, *125*
Tourette, Gilles de la, 40
Tourette's syndrome, 40–42
Transmogrification, 39
Transylvania, 55, 74, 76, 78, 81

"Undead," 56, 60, 63, 64, *64*, 69, 71, 82, 98

Vadadaire, Charles, 34–35
Vampire(s), 2, 9, 10, 23, 55, *63*, *66*, 86, 87; attacks, 68–69; and blood, 64; characteristics, 70–73; and the Church, 61–63; destroying, 65–66; and Dracula, 74–75, 81–83; legends, 55–56, 60–61; travel methods, 67; victims of, 74; warding off, 67
Vampire bat(s), 60, *61*
Vlad III, 76
Vlad IV. *See* Dracula, Vlad
Voodoo, 98, 124

Warne, Elizabeth, 50

Washington, George, 46
Walachia, 76, 79
Werewolf(ves), 2, 9, 22, 61, 70, 71, 86, *88*, *91*, *93*, *94*, 116, *165*; definition, 83; description, 87, 92; disease, 90–94, 96; medical treatment, 88–90; movies, 83, 85, 96; trials, 97
Willard, Samuel, 43–45, 48, 51
Winthrop, John, 49
Witch(es), 2, 8–10, 51, 71, 97, 101, 103, 106, 108, *117*, *119*, *128*, *132*, *134*, *139*, *140*, *142*, *143*, *145*, 150, 177; "cakes," 122, 129; curses, 57, 99; dark skin, 124; familiars, *102*, *115*; flying, 116; love potions, 99; persecution, 108–9, 111, 114, 116, 118–19, 136; spectral evidence, 118, 129; of today, 141–44
Witchcraft, 49, 50, 85, 105–6, 137–38, 141, 144; Black Mass, 108; books about, 114, 116; covens, 112–14; hunts, 100; legends, 97–99; sabbats, 106–7, 113–14; trials, 48, 52, 87, 121–34
Witchcraft Act, 118, 143
Witch doctor(s), 142
Wolf(ves), 85; howling, 86
Wolfsbane, 67

Yugoslavia, legends, 65–67

Zodiac, 150, 156, 160, 161, 163
Zombie(s), 98

AARON E. KLEIN taught life sciences in secondary schools and colleges for over ten years. Born in Atlanta, Georgia, he was educated in public schools in Georgia and Connecticut, the universities of Pennsylvania and Bridgeport, and Yale and Wesleyan universities. He participated in the Visiting Scientist Program of the Museum of Art, Science, and Industry in Bridgeport, Connecticut, and was managing editor of *Current Science* magazine. He has written many science books for young readers and adults and now lives in Connecticut.